What Advance Rea(... ~~·ut~~

WALKINC

LE&&ON& LEARNED w..

"Readers will laugh and cry—I certainly did! Mrs. Irwin's reflec..
are deep and always focus on glory to God. She shows how God
interacts with us, how His instruction and His wisdom have such
impact on our lives. She richly connects Sage's journey through life
and God's path for us. I will be rereading and reflecting on each
chapter to deepen my walk with God!"

~ KARI NORDAHL, BIBLE STUDY FACILITATOR AND ELEMENTARY SCHOOL EDUCATOR,
SAN BERNARDINO, CA

"The author's humble voice and the lessons she learned from her
beloved, blind canine friend are perfect for those times when you
need a little pick me up. Encouraging, uplifting, instructive and just
plain fun to read!"

~ TERRY WINSHIP, CEO, TRUE CARE WOMEN'S RESOURCE CENTER,
CASPER, WY

"The author's delight in how the Lord revealed His love through
Sage is infectious and a breath of fresh air! With vulnerability Gayle
shares how the Holy Spirit guides, reveals and heals the broken
heart. Sage is a wounded healer! Gayle's discernment and acute
awareness with respect to the intimacy between humans, God, and
animals is inspiring and encouraging. I commend this book as a
personal devotional, short daily readings, and as a resource for
encouragement and reality checks for anyone."

~ REVEREND FRANK KINNEY, RETIRED PRESBYTERIAN PASTOR
NEW HAMPSHIRE

"Mrs. Irwin's knowledge, understanding and love of the Bible permeate the whole history of her life with Sage. An inspiring work!"

~ ELIZABETH MARTIN, AUTHOR OF SAHRA'S QUEST AND MONAHAN'S SEARCH,
NATIVE OF SCOTLAND

"*Walking In Trust* is a very inspiring book! The author's blind dog,
Sage, is a true testimony to living by faith and not by sight. I
thoroughly enjoyed reading this book!"

~ TEKLA "BRANDI" DAY, BIBLE STUDY LEADER AND CHRIST AMBASSADOR,
CASPER, WY

WALKING IN TRUST

Lessons
Learned
with my
Blind Dog

GAYLE M. IRWIN

CLADACH
Publishing

Published by CLADACH Publishing
Greeley, Colorado www.CLADACH.com

Printed in the U.S.A.

ISBN-10: 0981892965
ISBN-13: 9780981892962

Table of Contents

Amazing grace, how sweet the sound
That saved a wretch like me;
I once was lost, but now I'm found,
Was blind, but now I see.

–John Newton, 1772

Introduction

"I have bad news for you. Your dog is going blind."

Those words spoken by the veterinarian that cold February day shot through me like a bullet, ricocheting from my stomach to my heart and mind. Dr. Johnson discovered progressive retinal atrophy (PRA), a genetic disease of the eye for which there is no cure. Within two years my dog would be completely blind in both eyes.

My husband, Greg, and I had recently decided to add a dog to our newly-married life. We liked the English springer spaniel's medium size and devoted, easy-going personality. Deciding to look for one in a local shelter (My heart breaks for the numerous pets that are separated from their people, especially those millions that wind up in shelters that euthanize animals—I can barely watch those ASPCA commercials on TV!), we didn't find any springers there. Then my mother called to say that there was a purebred female springer named Sage, only one-and-a-half years old, advertised through a shelter near her home in Montana, the Pet Assistance League.

Although Sage was available for adoption, she was still living in her human family's home. With a divorce pending, the woman preferred to keep Sage at the house until a new family adopted her. So we took the drive and visited Sage's home.

We found Sage to be an elegant dog; feathery fur wafted from her three-quarter length tail. Black spots, small and large, dotted her snowy coat. One big black spot saddled her side. This area beckoned to be petted, and I obliged. Her fur danced in wisps as Greg and I stroked her softness. She raised her long, black muzzle, and that's when I noticed something odd: she was staring at the ceiling.

The woman said, "Sage is a sweet dog—a bit spacey, but sweet."

"What do you mean?" I asked, glancing at my husband.

"Well, she stares at the ceiling—like she's doing now—or at the floor sometimes. She's a great dog, though—very loving and affectionate."

After twenty minutes, Greg and I left to discuss the adoption. I was hesitant; he was not.

"That's the dog for us!"

"What's up with the staring?"

"I don't know, maybe curiosity. It doesn't matter. I like that dog."

I relented. She was beautiful and sweet. And she needed a home. So, Montana Sage became Wyoming Sage on January 28, 2001.

Soon my husband and I noticed Sage doing other odd things. She would bump into furniture, stumble on the back porch steps, and balk at climbing our stairs. After a few months of this, we knew something was amiss. We decided to take her to the vet.

When I ran my hands down Sage's lean body, I could feel her quiver with nervousness. This was her first visit to Dr. Johnson's office with its strange smells and sounds. I looked at Sage's graying eyes. We hadn't given thought to the discoloration before, but as Dr. Johnson explained the course of this PRA disease, it dawned on me: the normal blackness appeared murky; a milky film covered part of the eyeball. Dr. Johnson estimated she still had about fifty percent of her vision in one eye and about seventy percent in the other. But he warned that within a few years she'd completely lose her vision.

Dumbfounded, Greg and I went home and researched how to best live with a blind dog. There would be challenges; but we had committed to caring for this dog, and we determined to make the best of a difficult situation.

Many friends questioned our decision to keep her.

"Can't you return her to the shelter and exchange her for a different dog?" some asked.

"Why don't you have her euthanized?" others added.

I admit, questions nagged my own mind. How will we ever adjust to living with a blind dog? And how will Sage adjust to the loss of sight?

At that time I couldn't imagine the wonderful lessons Sage would teach me, through her blindness, about life and about trusting God. Despite a springer's typically-happy personality, the loss of sight can bring despondency, especially to those animals that have previously experienced sight. I was impressed that, as Sage's sight lessened, one thing never waned—her wagging tail. She became an inspiration, not only to me but also to countless children and adults who met her.

Sage was both a teacher and a pupil. She and I learned from each other. At times, however, I believe I learned more from Sage than she did from me: lessons about trust, courage, loyalty, contentment, and perseverance. Come walk with Sage and me, and experience these—and other—lessons with us.

"Where am I?"
Sage in 2001, soon after being adopted by the Irwins

Sage experiences a new trail

Wandering and wondering
Making discoveries in the forest near the cabin

1
Courage

Be strong and courageous. Do not be terrified, do not be discouraged, for the LORD your God will be with you wherever you go.
—Joshua 1:9

On this Friday evening, Greg and I pack our tent and our dog (who is now completely blind) into the car. We're going for a campout on our newly-acquired property in the mountains outside of Casper, Wyoming. Six weeks ago we searched the classified section of the newspaper, found this land, and embarked upon our dream of owning mountain property and establishing a cabin. We feel blessed to have a one-and-a-half-acre parcel only twenty minutes from our community. We can stay overnight on a weeknight and still be able to get to work the next morning without much fuss. We are excited and dream-filled!

Only three hours after closing on the real-estate deal, we head out of Casper, drive fifteen miles up a winding paved road, find the turnoff to the dirt road, and travel down a small jeep trail to our property. We set up the tent, pull out the cook stove, and feast on hamburgers and potato chips. We gaze at millions of stars in a night sky undimmed by city lights or backyard torches. Away from noise pollution, this is simply tranquil. It's all natural—and it's ours!

In the morning, Sage lets me know she needs to go out, so I unzip the tent and let her step outside to get her job done. I simply lie back down in the sleeping bag and plan to doze for just a few more moments. I removed her collar last night because the jingle of the ID and rabies tags kept me awake.

About twenty minutes later, Greg wakes up, leaves the tent briefly, then sticks his head back in and asks, "Where's Sage?"

"Oh, I let her go out a bit ago. She's out there."

"No, Gayle, she's not."

Then I see Sage's collar sitting in the tent. I had neglected to put it back around her neck before letting her out!

I get dressed and we go looking for Sage. We spend hour after hour looking for her. The hours stretch into a day, and continue to a second miserable day. Friends offer to help us by walking, driving, posting flyers, and visiting campgrounds and cabins in the area. My throat becomes raw from calling Sage's name, talking to people, and crying. Neither my husband nor I voice our fears of what could have happened to Sage. We picture her falling down a hillside, being hit by a car, or getting mauled by a bear or mountain lion. Then, on the second night, a friend comes to our campsite to let us know that someone has seen a dog matching Sage's description—nearly two miles away. Sage is still alive!

At 6:30 a.m. the third morning, we have enough day-light to start searching. Sleeplessness and anxiety are etched on our faces like carvings in stone, as we walk the loop of clay and gravel roadway. Greg and I walk nearly thirty minutes, each taking a different fork in the road, wearied and worried with not having seen any sign of our dog. I

come upon a cabin where a woman is sweeping the porch.
As I tell her about our plight, with my back to the path, the
woman becomes distracted by something behind me.

"Is that the dog you're talking about?" she asks.

I turn around and see our beloved Sage running along
the road.

"Sage!" I yell.

She doesn't run to me; she runs away. Shocked by her
negative response to my voice, I chase her, still yelling her
name.

Greg hears me and jogs from his search site.

"What?! What is it?"

"Sage! I saw her, but she ran away from me."

We head in the direction I last saw her. We notice paw
prints in the dirt and little mud puddles created by last
evening's rain shower.

"Sage is probably incredibly scared," Greg whispers.
"Let's keep our voices low. And when we find her, don't yell
at her; that probably only scares her more."

"How will we get her back then?"

"We'll figure that out when the time comes."

Twenty minutes later we discover her sitting in a ditch
off the roadway, panting heavily. Greg motions for me to
stop and we gaze at our wayward dog for a moment. Terror
and uncertainty reflect in her unseeing eyes as her head
moves back and forth.

"We're going to have to sneak up on her," Greg whispers.
"You stay here, on the road, and I'll circle around her. I'll try
to grab her around the neck. If I miss, and she slips away
from me, you'll have to block her way and grab her."

"I don't know—"

"It's about our only chance, Gayle." My husband looks
determined.

I nod my head and wait as Greg detours and encircles

Sage from the right. He then cuts left, down the hill, moving slowly, and as silently as possible in a forest floor littered with downed timber and logs. I watch as my stealthy husband tiptoes toward Sage, who continues to sit panting in the ditch. Just as Greg comes within a breath of her, reaching his right arm towards her neck, Sage's head snaps his direction and she jumps to all four feet, ready to spring forward and away from his extended hand. Greg senses her leap and, like a football player on the field, tackles her, grabbing her body with his left arm and closing his right hand on the nape of her neck. I run down the hill toward them and I hear Greg, in as calm a voice as he can muster, saying Sage's name over and over. I kneel beside him, collar in my right hand. I whisper her name as well. Greg motions for me to give Sage's collar to him.

We both pet and talk to her, saying her name several times and telling her, "It's okay, girl. You're all right. It's us. You're safe."

The terror in her eyes nearly breaks my heart. Then, within a few short moments, a flicker of recognition replaces that terror. Sage listens to her name, spoken gently, listens to our soothing voices, and listens to our words of reassurance. Another few moments pass and then:

Bark! Bark! Woof! Woof!

Sounds of happiness resound from our once-lost, now-found dog, and she wiggles with relief and joy! Sage washes our faces and hands with licks of love and gratitude, and tears freely pour from our faces as Greg and I hug one another and voice our thanksgiving to God.

Although there were times during our search when we experienced doubt about whether we would find our wandering, roaming dog, we did pray to find her; God knew that great desire of our hearts. He also knew the fears that coagulated within our minds. He answered our prayer for Sage's

safekeeping and for our ability to find her, and we recognized
his guidance in this terrifying situation.

Greg and I were not the only ones facing fears at this
time. Sage was lost for two complete days and nights, from 7
a.m. on Saturday to 8 a.m. on Monday. A blind dog lost in the
woods faces unimaginable dangers, including downed timber,
rolling hillsides, rocks and boulders, and large carnivores that
can snatch and eat a sighted dog, let alone one that cannot see
such predators approaching.

I have been lost in the woods twice in my life, once as a
child and once as an adult. The first time I became lost took
place when I was seven years old and, like Sage, I wandered
from my parents while visiting a forested area. The second
time I became lost was at age twenty-four, attempting to take
a short cut to my parents' cabin in western Montana. I was
just as scared at age twenty-four as I was at age seven. Yet, I
was able to see. I can only imagine what terror Sage must have
felt wandering so far from her people, unable to see where she
was going, unable to hear familiar voices, blindly stumbling
over logs, into trees and branches, perhaps even rolling down
a hillside. She had gone out of range of the voices that usually
guided her back to safety.

I know fear. This dark emotion has been my friend, or
should I say my foe, many times in the past. I've been afraid
of losing someone I loved, not necessarily due to death, but
because of rejection. At nineteen, I was in love, engaged and
then abandoned; that fear of rejection haunted me for many
years. I've been afraid of not making enough money to pay
bills and buy groceries, especially when I teetered on the brink
of bankruptcy after a divorce. I've been afraid of not being
liked or respected, afraid of making changes—in essence,
afraid of the path I can't see.

Yet, Scripture encourages me, commands me actually,
to be courageous. God told Joshua to "be strong and

courageous." The angels announced "Fear not!" when they visited the shepherds on the night of Jesus' birth; God used the same words when he instructed Moses to go before Pharaoh. God also told Jeremiah not to fear. And Jesus encouraged his followers not to fear. "I tell you, my friends, do not be afraid of those who kill the body and after that can do no more," he says in Luke 12:4, and later, in verse 32, he says, "Do not be afraid, little flock, for your Father has been pleased to give you the kingdom."

All these Scriptures about fear, and commands to not be afraid, tell me that fear is something commonplace in the human spirit, and that courage is something I not only need, but can also attain. My mind knows what the Bible says; but my heart sometimes allows fear to take root and entrench itself into the depths of my being, consuming the nutrients of my faith much as weeds rob water and nutrients from garden soil.

Greg and I travel frequently to Montana to visit my parents. One particular night I was driving the car on Interstate-90, approaching the Montana state line from northern Wyoming. Darkness enveloped me like dense, thick smoke. The pitch black of the night surrounded the car in an almost tangible way. The further I drove the more that outside darkness caused a shroud of fear to overwhelm my mind and make me tense. Every fiber of my being was on high alert.

I had not been concerned about night driving until very recently. In my thirties, I often drove at night as part of my job as a newspaper editor, reporter and all-around journalist. Though I was conscientious in my driving then, watching for wildlife and oncoming vehicles, I wasn't fearful. This particular night, nearly fifteen years later, I was not just afraid. I was terrified! My sweating palms clutched the steering wheel. My knuckles tightened around it in a death grip. I was sure my heart would jump from my chest due to the intense pounding. My eyes darted back and forth, scanning the darkness for oncoming headlights and animals in the roadway. My fear was unexplainable yet overwhelming.

Scripture says our fight is against the powerful evil of a darkened world (see Ephesians 6:12), and that night I felt as though a war was raging for my sanity as darkness seeped into my soul like inky tar.

I eventually pulled the car over and let my husband finish that leg of our journey. Although I was no longer at the wheel, fear still gripped me like a vise. I watched diligently for deer along the interstate; kept an eye unwaveringly on the white line on the right side of the road; and watched with dread for oncoming traffic in our lane. I began to question my sanity. What is wrong with me?! I prayed earnestly, "Lord, help us. Protect us. Lord, take this unexplainable fear from me."

He didn't answer immediately. But during the next few hours of our journey I continued to whisper a word of prayer whenever the vise of dread squeezed me. Over the course of several hundred miles, tension subsided and we arrived safely at our destination. I found relief in calling out to God for assistance, and through his Holy Spirit he helped me relinquish my fears to him.

Like the cowardly lion in *The Wizard of Oz*, I had no courage that night. And God did not respond like the wizard, giving me a magic potion or a medal of courage to instantly make my life better. God has never been a genie for me, although that's what I've often asked of him. Through many harrowing scenarios in my life, from rejection to dejection, I've wanted those situations to change *now*. I've asked God for instant miracles or instant resolution, much like setting cold oatmeal in a microwave and having a warm breakfast in seconds.

The devil uses fear to try to dilute my faith. When I feel prone to fear, whether financial, medical, or spiritual, I try to recall God's many promises and the words of the psalmist who wrote, "The LORD is with me; I will not be afraid. What can mere mortals do to me?" (Psalm 118:6).

Fear is a prison of darkness. Like Sage running wildly through a forested area she could not see, when I'm afraid, I run blindly into obstacles of bad judgment, careless decisions, and emotional upheaval. The darkness of fear conjures up terrifying images—big, black monsters of negative thoughts and emotions leading me through gloomy tunnels in which I can get lost. Courage dissolves in the murky maze of fear. The only way out is God's way—leaning on him and allowing him to guide me, instead of piloting myself or letting my faulty thoughts and changing emotions lead me astray.

If fear is a prison, then faith unlocks the cell doors of fear. I know that God provides and protects despite what lurks along the highways of life. Nothing is impossible with God. Despite all the odds against our finding Sage alive and unharmed, we did. And that night on the interstate, just as in the days and nights spent searching for Sage, I asked God to direct our path, to sustain us and to keep us safe. I didn't understand the foreboding fear threatening to engulf me that night traveling to Montana. I needed to lean on the Lord. God heard and answered my prayer, not only keeping us safe from highway harm and keeping Sage from the jaws of death on the mountain, but also bringing to mind reassuring verses from the Bible. Though the devil wanted fear to overtake my mind and my heart, the Holy Spirit responded by outshining the shadows in my soul.

Being mindful of God's multitude of promises and know-ing that nothing can separate me from his love—neither darkness nor demons, nor anything above, in, or below the Earth (see Romans 8:38-39)—helps me live with greater courage, just as my blind dog showcased courage every time she sauntered down the sidewalk or reached out a paw to climb a staircase she could not see.

Sage rebounded from her ordeal of being lost in the woods. She sustained only small cuts on her face and legs, probably from tree limbs and fallen timber. She continued to do the same things she would do if she weren't blind: wagging her tail, running through the backyard chasing birds and squirrels, traveling to strange places and meeting new people, jumping onto the bed and the chair for a nap.

We will never know what transpired for Sage on that mountain during those fateful August days and nights. Blind, lost, scared, hungry, thirsty, and stressed, Sage wandered and probably wondered if she would ever find her home and her people again. But that experience did not scar her. She constantly walked in darkness, but she did not continue to walk in fear. She may not have physically seen light, yet she knew light. Her light was my presence and my voice. She trusted me to call her back from potentially-bad situations, such as straying too far off the sidewalk. Her reliance on me as her guide allowed her to live courageously. Like Sage, I, too, rely upon the One who loves and guides but whom I cannot see. Just as Sage bravely lived and survived despite the darkness surrounding her, I, too, can walk through and live in a spiritually-darkened world. God's light of love and grace illuminate my path, keeping me from being overwhelmed by the darkness of fear.

PRAYER:
Heavenly Father, thank you for your Holy Spirit that helps me face my fears. Thank you for your promises and your Word that calm my fears. Thank you for your love that guides my every step. May I always remember that I am yours, that you have great plans for me, and that I can do all things through Christ because you, oh God, are my strength! Amen.

2
Patience

I waited patiently for the L ord; he turned to me and heard my cry.
—Psalm 40:1

I lead Sage around our living room, encouraging her to let her body brush against the furniture, like a gentle paint stroke on canvas. Her wavy fur touches the sofa, the recliner, the entertainment center. We pause by each item; I pick up her right leg and lightly pat her paw on the piece of furniture. I recall the instructions of our vet, Dr. Johnson, guidelines to help Sage adjust to her impending blindness. It requires repetition, and that repetition requires patience.

As Sage and I repeat our route through the living room, she doesn't pull away. Instead she patiently endures the repeated procedure of walking diligently through all the rooms in the house. Without complaint she allows me to raise her foot and tap it against the table in the dining room, on the bed in our bedroom, and on the desk and futon in the guest room. For an hour we continue this furniture association.

We take a break in the backyard. Lilac and mock-orange sweeten the spring air, and leaves just-sprouted on the trees flutter in the breeze. I release Sage from her leash; immediately the two-year-old English springer spaniel runs from the security of my side and leaps into the air (normal behavior for springers!). As she gallops through the yard, a squirrel chatters from the cottonwood tree. Sage's keen ears fall forward, savoring the sound and anticipating a tasty treat. She turns and races toward the screech as if the tree wasn't there.

"Sage!" I give a warning yell, hoping to steer her from her collision course. But I am too late.

Smack! Whack! Sage's head crashes into the tree, the impact knocking her to the ground. I run to her and kneel beside her. Sage slowly regains her footing, shakes her head, and barks. She runs circles around the tree, woofing the entire time, as if scolding the squirrel for the mishap. I re-hook her leash to her collar and we stroll outside, taking care to circumvent the big cottonwood tree that dominates the center of the yard. Although she stays beside me for the next forty-five minutes, she tugs a few times, wanting to run free again. I keep her reined in and repeat our backyard route several times, as I teach Sage where the various bushes and trees stand in our yard and where the chain link and wooden fences are located. She takes these repetitive lessons in stride and sniffs with interest each place we stop.

A tedious exercise! But Dr. Johnson's words of wisdom resound in my mind. He said the routine and repetition would be helpful for Sage. He suggested that we not rearrange our furniture and that we should walk Sage on the same route every day, to help her memorize her environment. He termed it "cognitive mapping." Sounds great. But the process requires fortitude—for me and for Sage.

Patience is a virtue, so the saying goes. Many circumstances require us to exercise this virtue—with ourselves, other people, and situations. According to Galatians 5:22, patience is a gift of the Holy Spirit. But it's a gift I failed to unwrap for many years, like a present still sitting forgotten under the Christmas tree. It doesn't take much to dissolve my serenity, to needle my heart, mind and spirit. Writing deadlines, computers and washing machines breaking down, pets becoming ill, and vehicles needing repair: juggling these tangled situations creates stress and frustration within me.

Only through the power of the Holy Spirit can I unwrap the gift of patience. Jesus promised, "And I will ask the Father, and he will give you another advocate to help you and be with you forever—the Spirit of truth" (John 14:16-17). As I continue in my faith walk and the Spirit develops God's fruit within me, patience is part of the package. I unwrap it slowly and deliberately, savoring the sweetness of ripened fruit.

Living with a special-needs dog presented opportunities to learn endurance. All dogs require training, at least simple commands such as "off" and "no." Some dog owners teach obedience with hand signals, but because of Sage's blindness, we used verbal commands. The repetition of walking the same route and being coached as to the layout of the inside and outside of the house also served as a strong teaching tool. Both instructor and student needed patience with this process. The Apostle Paul instructed Timothy to "correct, rebuke and encourage—with great patience and careful instruction" (see 2 Timothy 4:2). Patience is not always an easy crop to cultivate, but it reaps a great harvest. Sage never again ran into the cottonwood tree, and I developed a greater palate of fortitude.

My mother used to plant a large garden every year, and growing up I enjoyed the fruits of her labor—strawberries, tomatoes, watermelon, corn, all succulent and sweet. Just as my mother persistently planted, then later harvested food crops for our family, through patience, I cultivated an endearing relationship with my blind dog that ultimately helped me grow in my walk with God.

"Be still before the LORD and wait patiently for him," writes the Psalmist (Psalm 37:7). Waiting is not always easy. Neither is being still. In today's fast-paced world, I encounter instant messaging, on-the-spot news casts, pre-packaged foods, and so many other "instant gratification" products. I am bombarded with "instantaneous" when I should be producing patience. Just as my mother did not expect the seeds to sprout instantly or to harvest bushels of bounty within moments, I cannot expect all things to be right in my life immediately. Although God could answer my prayers and petitions instantly, he doesn't text me with an immediate response to my request nor does he wave a magic wand over my life and make the little annoyances or big problems vanish. Microwaved answers do not teach trust.

Less than two years after Greg and I adopted her, Sage went completely blind. During that time, Sage learned to trust those who cared for her; she also learned to trust herself. That took time, and it took staying power. My husband and I could have given up on her and on ourselves; some people would have taken Sage back to an animal shelter. Sage also could have stopped trying, huddling in a corner or in her kennel. However, patience with herself, her caregivers, and her circumstances prevailed in my blind dog.

Sage walked in darkness most of her life. Humans, too, walk through a spiritually-darkened world, facing trying circumstances and difficult people. Patience is needed to meander through the maze of life. Wounding words and destructive deeds, as well as lack of communication and common sense, can cause frustration and anger. But Solomon says, "A person's wisdom yields patience; it is to one's glory to overlook an offense" (Proverbs 19:11). It takes the work of the Holy Spirit to serve up patience instead of annoyance.

The Apostle Paul reminds me that even when the situation is difficult, we may be "strengthened with all power according to his glorious might so that (we) may have great endurance and patience" (Colossians 1:11). From small annoyances like ineffective computers or late dinner guests to major challenges such as health issues and the death of loved ones, cultivating the crop of patience reaps a harvest of calmness, contentment and strength. This is a lesson that I continually need to apply.

God himself is patient. The Apostle Peter says, "The LORD is not slow in keeping his promise, as some understand slowness. Instead he is patient with you" (2 Peter 3:9). God patiently guides my life, just as I methodically guided Sage in those early days and for many years thereafter. He also waits for me when I travel off-course, just as Sage waited for me to return from work. I am truly thankful that God is patient, even when I am not!

Sage's patience helped her deal with lack of sight. Despite intermittent knocks into trees and walls, she navigated the house and backyard. She would search for me until she found me, maneuvering her way from the bedroom to the living room or from the living room to my office. She never tired of running through the backyard, chasing and barking at a squirrel she smelled and heard but could not see. Her blindness did not thwart her endeavor or her spirit.

PRAYER:
When little annoyances pile up like a ton of bricks and weigh me down, or when big boulders hit me hard, when patience seems like the last virtue I can muster, I remember the special dog that would lie patiently at my feet, and I recall the words from Scripture to 'be still before the LORD and wait patiently for him.'

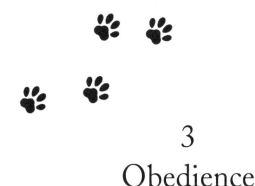

3
Obedience

We demolish arguments and every pretension that sets itself up against the knowledge of God, and we take captive every thought to make it obedient to Christ. –2 Corinthians 10:5

This June day dawns with layered colors of apricot, peach and cherry. Cottony clouds drift lazily, a light breeze rustles the new green leaves on the cottonwood trees. As Sage and I stroll through our neighborhood, the sleepy street reflects the silence of the morning. This is one of our favorite times to share together—peaceful and warm, no distractions. We approach the park laced with playground equipment and picnic tables then turn onto a dirt path leading to the bridge that crosses the creek. The leash in my hand helps guide my blind dog along the walkway, preventing her from straying off the bridge. Snowmelt from the sun's warmth creates a fast-moving torrent in the usually slow, meandering stream. I keep the leash short and taut as we walk up the hill to keep her from slipping off the side and falling into the creek below. I allow her to sniff the trees and shrubs but keep her moving so we can return home in time for me to get ready for work.

At the end of our twenty-minute nature-trail walk, we still have ten minutes to walk around the block. We prepare to cross the street. Though traffic is quiet, I pull Sage's leash tighter.

"Stop," I command.

Sage stops.

I look both ways, just as children are taught to do. Before crossing the street I tell my dog, "Step down." We step off the curb together. On the other side, I command, "step up."

She lifts her foot to the curb.

Our early-morning walk continues. We repeat this scenario again before returning home.

During our thirty-minute journey, we hear chickadees chirp and squirrels chatter. Last night raindrops pelted our community, but the morning sky is clear, the air fresh and crisp. Although Sage enjoys hearing and smelling the myriads of morning sounds and scents, she also listens and responds to my commands. She would be easily distracted, and find it difficult to listen to me, if she weren't tethered to me.

Because the weather forecast calls for a sunny day with a high of seventy degrees, I decide Sage can stay outdoors while Greg and I are gone to work. We have lived in this house for two years, and Sage is quite familiar with the layout, not only of the rooms, but also of the backyard. Wooden and chainlink fencing surrounds our property and keeps her confined. Sage has never attempted to leave the yard. She finds many things to occupy her time when she's not resting, such as chasing squirrels and sniffing the fence line, filling her nose with the many scents that flourish in a yard near a creek. A lilac bush and other shrubs scattered throughout the enclosure offer shade from the early summer sun.

Still led by the leash, Sage follows me to the back door.

"Step down," I command.

She steps down from the doorway onto the concrete step.

"Step down," I say again.

Again she steps from the cement onto the grass below. In the yard I unhook the leash. "Go!"

What does my blind dog do now? She bounds away from the patio, barking with enthusiasm and freedom. She runs a lap around the circumference of our large yard, deftly avoiding the trees and shrubs. I watch a moment, basking in Sage's joy as she leaps high into the air like a "normal" springer. I fill her water dish and set it down in a shady spot. I clap my hands and call her name, encouraging her to come to me. She obliges. I then remind her where the water dish is located by hooking one of my fingers under her collar and leading her to the spot. Sage takes a short drink and returns to her joyful frolic through the yard, running in circles around the large cottonwood tree that grows almost directly in the center of our outdoor space.

When Sage first came to live with us, the tree was a hindrance to her freedom in those times where her body collided into it. However, the enormous tree later shaded her during the afternoon and provided hours of entertainment as well as nesting areas for birds and squirrels that she could smell. She would run around that towering tree, barking loudly, as a squirrel watching from a low branch would chatter and scold. Sage responded to her bushy-tailed neighbors by circling and barking some more.

In the backyard, she enjoyed outdoor freedom from the leash: leaping, running, barking, sniffing, resting, chasing, eating or drinking. Whatever Sage felt like doing, she did. The confinement may have represented a set of rules, but within the boundaries of those rules Sage found comfort because she was kept safe. There was a freedom that came with obedience; for by obeying my command to "come" or to "stop," Sage was kept safe—from traffic, from collisions with trees and fences, even from other dogs or wildlife. There was a time for the leash, being closely guided, and there was a time for freedom within the confines of the yard. However, complete unbounded freedom could lead to danger, or worse.

If Sage ignored the commands we'd taught her—such as "sit," "stay," "come," "step up," and "step down"—her safety could be compromised, from being run over by a car to falling down a set of stairs.

Similarly, God has given commands to me for my benefit. If I am not obedient to those commands, I may misstep or encounter a tragic mishap that puts my physical or spiritual life in jeopardy.

It is for my own good that God expects me to listen and obey. Proverbs 1:33 says, "Whoever listens to me will live in safety and be at ease, without fear of harm." God told the Hebrew people nearly the same thing back in the days of Moses: "Now if you obey me fully and keep my covenant, then out of all nations you will be my treasured possession" (Exodus 19:5). The Old Testament mentions obedience often. But no matter how many times God broached the subject, the Hebrew people balked. "You must obey my laws and be careful to follow my decrees. I am the LORD your God," records Leviticus 18:4. There was major penalty for their disobedience.

Disobedience has taken place since Adam and Eve walked in the Garden of Eden. They ate of the tree God specifically instructed them to not eat from. Disobedience flows through human hearts like blood courses through arteries. Yet, disobedience does not bring life; it does not bring freedom. Disobedience brings death. "If you do not obey the LORD your God and do not carefully follow all his commands and decrees … all these curses will come on you and overtake you," records Moses in Deuteronomy 28:15.

Our eternal death is not God's desire. Jesus was sent to revoke the curse of sin. Jesus, the obedient servant, took the punishment for the disobedience of all humankind—from Adam and Eve to me, and to future generations.

Though I may argue with God as to why I don't want to obey him, his will is for my good, even if I can't see or understand the potential outcomes. Sage couldn't see the steps or curbs in front of her, but she knew that when she listened to and obeyed my commands of "step up" and "step down," she would be kept from tumbling down the steps or stumbling on the concrete. Sage trusted me to take care of her and to keep her from falling or being hurt. She may not have always wanted to obey—at times her self-control was overpowered by her strong will. But when she did obey my instructions, she was rewarded in some way, even if it just meant keeping her feet firmly planted on a solid object and not stepping off into some abyss.

One time she did fall down a chasm. Early one summer morning, Greg and I took her for a walk along the nature trail. As we returned, we decided to release Sage from the leash before we arrived at the park. We walked side-by-side, talking in low tones, enjoying the warmth at 6:30 a.m., listening to mallards quack and warblers trill. However, the silvery-pure tranquility suddenly tarnished into muck at the sound of: *Splash! Crash!*

Quickening our pace, we called Sage's name; but she didn't come. More splashing sounds arose from the creek below, and we knew by the weighty noise, they weren't duck splashes! Greg and I ran to the edge of the hill overlooking the creek. There below was our blind dog paddling in frantic circles. We yelled her name again and raced down to the water's edge. The pool was fairly deep, and Sage was able to swim; but she couldn't find the creek bank, and her feet could not touch the bottom. In her panic, she couldn't tell the direction of our voices.

Greg waded out into the creek, holding the dog leash

above the water, reaching for and grabbing her collar. Together, the two made their way to the grassy edge and pulled themselves out of the creek.

Sage shook water from her fur. Greg and I examined her and decided a trip to the vet wasn't warranted. So the three of us finished our walk. The warmth of the summer sun dried both Sage and Greg, but back in the security of home we toweled her down. Sage plopped on a rug near the large picture window, where the sun warmed and relaxed her body; and she soon fell asleep. We checked her again before leaving for work and again found no reason to call the vet, so off we went to our respective places of employment.

During that escapade, Sage found out that freedom could be fun for a while, but ultimately could be frightening and treacherous. Obviously, Greg and I should have kept closer vigil over her; we were still learning the parameters of being blind-dog owners.

That's something I never have to worry about with God; he is ever vigilant and he's a patient parent! "The LORD watches over you—the LORD is your shade at your right hand" (Psalm 121:5).

Sage wasn't disobeying when she ran off and fell into the stream, because we didn't call her back until after she had toppled from the cliff to the creek. But she did wander too far from the safety of her people.

I often wander off the path myself. In those times, it seems stubbornness can lead to waywardness, which can, in turn, propagate disobedience. I am willful at times. So was my dog on occasion. Although she responded well to "step up" and "step down," Sage didn't always "come" when called—especially if she was in the backyard barking at the neighbor dog or checking on the deer who curiously came close to her. Then even my tempting her with the promise of a "biscuit" didn't cause her to turn and "come" to me. When God calls me and instructs me to "come", there are times when I'm like my dog—I don't always listen. Instead, I go my own way, doing my own thing. I eventually do return, after realizing the consequences of not listening and not obeying the Father. Like the prodigal's father in the story about the wayward son (see Luke 15:11-31), my heavenly Father welcomes me back. But, oh, if I had only listened the first time, perhaps my head wouldn't have hit the tree or I wouldn't have fallen into the water-filled abyss that life presented to me.

One of God's special gifts is that of free will. I am free to choose to obey—or not. I am free to listen to the LORD—or not. Yet, danger lurks when I misuse my freedom, just like Sage experienced when she fell into the creek. I have found great freedom in walking closely with God. By doing so, and by obeying his promptings and commands, I enjoy greater peace and comfort because I am not struggling to try to control everything. By recognizing God's sovereignty and allowing him control over my life, his strength and guidance provide me with freedom and peace.

Jesus said he came to give people abundant life (see John 10:10). Sage and I both learned that there is joyful freedom within the bounds of obedience.

PRAYER:
Heavenly Father, thank you for the freedom that comes from knowing you and from obeying you. Help me, Holy Spirit, to become more obedient to your promptings, to God's Word and commandments, so I can follow in the footsteps of Jesus and experience that abundant life he came to give me.

"I clean up nice!"
Sage shows off her new summer haircut.

"Singing" and barking at those pesky squirrels

4
Forgiveness

Bear with each other and forgive whatever grievances you may have against one another. Forgive as the LORD forgave you. —Colossians 3:13

On this soggy spring morning I awaken early, groggy after a restless night. The sky is gray and clouds lie low over the mountains to the south. Moisture is visible on the sidewalks, and rain continues to fall steadily. The dreary weather mirrors my mood. I lament the fact that I am turning forty-five. I sit in my recliner, staring blankly for a moment as my brooding mind turns dark pages from the book of my life. The most recent recollection involves struggles with a co-worker who seems to have issues with several others as well. Our work environment is tense and testy, causing me great distress. Continuing through that tunnel of trouble, another colleague-related challenge comes to mind. That time it was the manager who caused upheaval within the organization. Further furrows of strife engage my brain and heart. I think about how I was engaged at nineteen but betrayed at twenty; how I fell deeply in love again at thirty-four only to lose that love because of my obsession and insecurity; how I wasted too much of my life wandering and worrying.

Conflict grows within my mind as I listen to the accusations bombarding me. (These lies may come from the enemy, my own thinking, or messages I received during my youth):

You've failed.

You're not lovable.

You're not good enough.

Look at what they did to you.

Look at what you let them do.

I fall deeper into a trap of turmoil, allowing resentment toward myself and those who hurt me to build like lava in a Hawaiian volcano. Flipping through those pages of my life's story, losses loom like the Himalayas in my mind's eye, and anger storms the walls of my heart.

Suddenly, those pages flutter away like a newspaper in the wind as I feel a pat on my leg. Sage has awakened, jumped out of bed and sought me out. Though I had been sitting silent, she uses her nose to track me down, and she rousts me from my early morning reviling reminiscences.

There is her paw on my leg again. I reach down to pat her head. But a slight pat doesn't satisfy Sage. She scratches at the recliner, and I help her climb up. She curls up near me, and lets out a sigh of satisfaction. Laying her head on my lap, my blind dog snuggles against me and closes her eyes for a few more moments of early morning rest. My hand on her head, I begin to stroke her soft wavy fur. Doing so quells the voice of disappointment and dissatisfaction vibrating in my heart and mind. I reflect upon my dog's life instead of my own, recalling the number of times Sage hit her head on a table, a corner of a room, or even a tree. Had she been disappointed at herself or even angry at the object in her path? No. She simply shook her head and moved on. Eventually, she found her way around the problem and got to where she was supposed to be. Remembering Sage's many stumbles and struggles, I shake the convoys of condemnation from my mind.

The positive moments in my life present themselves to my mind, from when I was a seven-year-old girl lost in the woods and found at last, to being found by God as I wandered lost in my life at age thirty-seven. And images of many friends flash in my mind—people I might not have met had it not been for the pathway I took.

I then recall some of the incredible experiences in my life, such as living near Yellowstone National Park, countless camping and fishing trips, and the fun of traveling to Los Angeles to whale watch in the Pacific Ocean.

I think of: my parents and the encouragement and love they've given; my husband and his smiling face when he greeted me at the altar on our wedding day; the travels we've made together.

My forty-fifth birthday may have dawned with despair and discontent; however, God's gracious light shines in my life, thanks to the persistent pawing and soft sighing of a blind English springer spaniel, swinging me back around to the positive pathway of recalled blessings.

The regrets and recollections which rose to greet me that particular morning seemed inescapable. As I dwelt on past hurts and disappointments, I dug a well of unforgiveness. I slammed into the wall of my own heart by focusing on mistakes and pain either caused by me or done to me. I could not let go of the renewed feelings of hurt and betrayal, which had been safely hidden for years. I had secretly censored the scenes from my life, silently creating a shield of stone over my heart. Turning forty-five, and trying to deal with work-related personnel issues, broke the seal of that stone wall. It came tumbling down.

How many times had Sage hit a wall—literally? They were too numerous to count! Even when using the leash, if

I neglected to watch, and she would end up walking into a hedge, a fence, or even a solid brick retaining wall along the edge of a yard. The time Sage fell into the creek near our rental house, she could have blamed Greg and me for not keeping closer watch, or even for letting her run off-leash. Though at first she showed no signs of injury, later that day I returned home to find that Sage was not her usual self.

I hooked the leash to Sage's collar, and she stepped from the house into the backyard. We strolled to the fences and around the bushes. That's when I noticed something odd: her flag tail, which she usually held upright, now drooped. There seemed to be a crook at the base of Sage's spine. Greg and I monitored this for another day; but the flag did not wave as usual.

At the vet's office we described Sage's fall into the creek. The vet examined her back and the base of her tail. He found no broken bones, just bruising, and told us that Sage would mend very soon. He was right, for by week's end, Sage's beautiful, furry tail danced upright once again!

We were fortunate that the fall was not more serious for Sage, who could have been badly injured. We blamed ourselves for her slip from the dirt wall into the creek. We could have kept a better eye on her. We should have called her to us sooner instead of allowing her to venture into harm's way.

And sweet Sage's reaction? Although she slept a bit more that week, she never withdrew her affection or withheld her love from Greg and me because of our failures. She was quick to forgive us.

So it is with God. Scripture says, "The Lord is slow to anger, abounding in love and forgiving sin and rebellion" (Numbers 14:18). When I rebel and sin, even if unintentionally, I am always forgiven, if I seek the Lord's forgiveness; I have only to ask. 1 John 1:9 reminds us, "If we confess our sins, he is faithful and just and will forgive us our sins and purify us from all unrighteousness."

Sage forgave numerous blunders I made. I'd been guilty of stepping on her tail or foot and tripping over her in the kitchen. In turn, I forgave her for getting into the trash and the cats' litter boxes. Each "oops!" ended with hugs of mercy.

Mercy is not just for my dog; I am also to extend forgiveness to people. God expects me to forgive those who knowingly or unknowingly hurt me. Just as I sometimes stepped on Sage's toes, people I care about have stepped on mine. But, God calls me to be gracious and merciful, as he is. "Do not judge, and you will not be judged. Do not condemn, and you will not be condemned. Forgive, and you will be forgiven," Jesus instructs in Luke 6:37.

Not only do I need to forgive the wrongdoing at work today, but also the lost loves and betrayals of my yesterdays. If I harbor hurt from an infidelity twenty-five years ago, I may look at my husband's actions today with a cynical eye and chew on his words differently than he intended. Although I've told myself I've forgiven my former fiancé and had asked God many years ago to help me forgive, some word, some thought brings that image back to my mind and heart, and I seethe all over again. Although a few years have passed since I walked away from the best paying job I ever had, when financial struggles present themselves, I beat myself up emotionally for allowing one person to dictate the happenings (and my feelings) at that job. In that self-absorbed process, I am forgetting about the new doors God opened that have allowed me to work from home several days a week.

Jesus not only talked about forgiveness; he lived the example. His disciples abandoned him prior to the crucifix-ion. Peter even denied knowing him. Yet, after he had been beaten and mocked, and as he was hanging on the cross, he asked his heavenly Father to forgive all of them, including those who tortured and killed him. Jesus didn't call down the legions of angels that would have defended him. Instead, he spoke incredible words of prayer, asking the Father to forgive those people, since they didn't know what they were doing (see Luke 23:34).

Am I able to forgive someone who disdains me? Can I forgive those who hurt me—people who do some wrong against me? According to Scripture, I must. If I hold a grudge against someone and don't forgive him, then how can God forgive me of my sins? (See Mark 11:25.)

Sometimes the person I need to forgive is myself. Guilt can plague me if I allow it to take root. Yet, if I am truly repentant, I am assured of God's forgiveness. I don't have to beat myself up as I remember Jeremiah's prophecy that the Lord will forgive our wickedness and will no longer remember our sins (see Jeremiah 31:34). Earnestly seeking and receiving God's forgiveness gives me faith to forgive myself, believing that "as far as the east is from the west, so far has he removed our transgressions from us" (Psalm 103:12).

If I seek God's forgiveness sincerely and believe he has forgiven me but don't forgive myself, then my relationship with God is weakened because I am acting as if I don't really believe he could forgive me.

Forgiveness is not only beneficial for the one I've forgiven, but it also helps me. Harboring hurts keeps me from experiencing joy. Dwelling on disappointments and reveling in resentment keeps me suspicious of others, and leads me to a Polar region of a cold, negative attitude and disposition. Not forgiving others can lead to depression and stress, even high blood pressure and other physical, as well as emotional, ailments. Forgiveness cleanses. Forgiveness satisfies.

Forgiveness brings freedom.

I may have opened the poisonous pages of defeat on my forty-fifth birthday, but I closed them with absolution. I traveled out of turmoil thanks to the pawing and nudging of my sweet blind dog, who, with all her angst, could easily not have pardoned me—or herself for that matter. I may have started my birthday by reflecting on snippets of my autobiography, but with the Lord's help through the Bible and through the pawing of my blind dog, I began a fresh new chapter to my story.

PRAYER:

Heavenly Father, thank you for your forgiveness. Thank you that I can come to you in repentance and that you don't turn a blind eye or a deaf ear. You promise that when I seek your grace, I will find it. Help me to forgive others as you instruct me to do, remembering that forgiveness is also for the one who forgives.

5

Blameless

For the LORD God is a sun and shield; the LORD bestows favor and honor; no good thing does he withhold from those whose walk is blameless. –Psalm 84:11

Returning home from work, I unlock the front door and enter the hallway,

"Sage! I'm home!"

Only silence answers me. So I step into the living room. And what do I see? Stuffing!—couch stuffing scattered throughout the room. The polyfoam congregates like drifted snowflakes near the entertainment center. I stand staring in horror at a piece of furniture that once was a decent place for humans to sit, and upon which my dog used to rest. The tattered and ripped blue cushions sit in their usual place on the couch under the picture window, but now they look like a raging bull has raked its horns through the fabric.

Sage is nowhere in sight.

I yell her name, louder this time. My angry voice echoes through the small house as I search for her. In the bedroom I find Sage cowering in a corner. Her head hangs in shame. I scold her and she seems to understand. Her body quivers.

A few moments later, my husband returns from work.

He hears me calling out, "Bad dog, bad dog!" He follows my raised voice to the bedroom.

"Why are you getting after Sage? Why is she shaking?"

"Just look—see what's left of our couch?"

He stares at the destruction.

"What happened?!"

"Something obviously got into her. Maybe boredom—but I don't know."

We start cleaning up the mess. Sage sits in the corner of our bedroom like a disfavored child.

"We may have to crate her all day after this," I say, with heat in my voice. "We can't trust her."

We fill a garbage bag with the couch stuffing, and Greg puts the bulging bag in the trash. When he comes back in the house, a puzzled expression appears on his face, and in his hand is a piece of paper.

"What's that?" I ask.

"I found this on the back door." He hands the manila note to me.

With a brief glance I see it's from the phone company. I look at my husband, then back at the paper again.

"Seems as though we had visitors while we were gone," Greg says.

The paper states that a technician had been at our home earlier in the day to replace some old phone wiring. Then I remember that we had called the phone company last week to discuss background noise in the phone system.

"Maybe that's what set Sage off," Greg says. He steps out our back door and motions for me to follow. We discover our phone box is located on the backside of the house on the wall paralleling the sofa. Greg looks at me sadly. "I think I understand why Sage tore up the couch—"

"The repairman was here when we were not," I finish for him. "There was probably a lot of noise, and certainly a strange man's presence—maybe even an unfamiliar voice."

"She was probably pretty scared."

Together we go back into the house. Sage is lying in the far corner of our bedroom. We sit beside her and take turns talking softly to her, reassuring her that we are not mad. I feel terrible for getting after her so harshly.

"You must have been frightened, Little Girl," I say in a mothering tone. "I'm so sorry!"

Within moments, she responds to our calmer, loving tones with happy thumps of her tail against the floor. I place my face near hers, and she licks my cheek. Acceptance and relief replace her fear, disgrace and shame.

Sage was not the only one to know shame and disgrace. How many times have I blundered in my life? How often have I made bad choices to gossip, to not tell the complete truth, or to falter and fail in other ways? I've ripped my own couches in a manner of speaking, letting rage, fear or hurt overtake me. I know what it's like to have the stuffing ripped from my heart, to give a retaliatory response. But later I cower guiltily in a corner, afraid to face my failures and fears.

Like Sage, it's easier for me to stay in my corner of shame than to admit my error. However, Scripture tells me I don't have to stay in the corner. My disgrace and guilt are covered by Jesus' sacrifice. His blood atones for my sins. "The blood of Jesus ... purifies us from all sin" (1 John 1:7).

Because I'm human, I'm not perfect. Because this is a fallen world, I won't be perfect in this life. But when I acknowledge my faults and confess my wrongdoing to the heavenly Father, his forgiveness covers my errors like a blanket of new-fallen snow.

"Blessed is the one whose transgressions are forgiven, whose sins are covered" (Psalm 32:1).

Even though Sage destroyed the couch, I counted her

blameless because of the fright she must have felt with that stranger's voice and the probable pounding against the wall outside. I forgave her. Likewise, God looks upon me as blameless because of the cross of Christ.

I am called to be blameless before the Lord. However, I cannot do that in my own strength. Paul says "all have sinned and fall short of the glory of God"—but "righteousness is given through faith in Jesus Christ to all who believe … and all are justified freely by his grace through the redemption that came by Christ Jesus" (Romans 3:22-24). Just as I sought out Sage after her encounter with the couch, God seeks to redeem me from unrighteousness. According to the psalmist, when I've sincerely sought his forgiveness for what I've done wrong, I know that "as far as the east is from the west, so far has he removed (my) transgressions" (Psalm 103:12).

During Old Testament times, blood sacrifices were required for covering the sins of the Hebrew people. Bulls, lambs, and doves were slaughtered as blood atonement. Christ fulfilled that sacrifice, and I am thankful to be sanctified and purified by Christ's blood. How much more, then, will the blood of Christ, who through the eternal Spirit offered himself unblemished to God, cleanse our consciences from acts that lead to death, so that we may serve the living God! (Hebrews 9:14).

Just as I constantly need God's forgiveness, so did Sage need my grace. As a hunting breed, Sage's nose "knew" things, like meat remnants, boxes of crackers, and even cat litter boxes. If the garbage container was left out, she would raid whatever sacks or small cans her nose discovered. We learned to gate off the cat box area, to set small trash cans on shelves, and to have a metal garbage receptacle in the kitchen. Although I never understood the appeal of raiding litter boxes and stinky garbage, I forgave Sage if I came home and found pieces of Kleenex or cracker boxes littering my living room.

Someone had forgotten to put those things in their proper place—away from Sage's inquisitive nose and sharp teeth.

I'm sure God is saddened by the garbage in my life: the stink that comes from my words of anger, the putridness of envious thoughts, or the stench of my lack of compassion when I drive past a person with placard that reads "Out of Work, Out of Food." Yet, when I bring to the Lord all that trash and the rest of the garbage trailing through the rooms of my heart, he will sanctify me through and through and keep me blameless (see 1 Thessalonians 5:23).

Having a pure heart can only come through being blameless before God. In my humanness, I cannot be blameless any more than Sage could be blameless in her doggie-ness, as when she tipped over the trashcan or squeezed through the gate to get to the cat box. But when I approach God, seeking his grace, he cleanses me, making me pure and blameless once again. Purity in my thoughts, words and deeds comes only through the purity of Christ and the power of the Holy Spirit.

Sage's days of digging in the garbage or the cat litter box faded. When she was older, she was not the raiding soldier of stinky trash that she once was. Still, we kept our bathroom trash can on a shelf out of her reach. Just as young children like to play in mud and don't seem to outgrow that urge for many years, so it was with Sage. We remained cautious. It's easy for a dog to follow its nose to places it shouldn't go. And it's easy for me to follow the path of putridity instead of purity.

PRAYER:
Lord, may your Holy Spirit guide my thoughts, words and deeds along the path of purity so that I can be blameless in your sight because of the blood sacrifice of your Son, Jesus. Thank you for the gift of grace that cleanses me.

6
Mystery

Now to him who is able to establish you by my gospel and the proclamation of Jesus Christ, according to the revelation of the mystery hidden for long ages past, but now revealed and made known through the prophetic writings by the command of the eternal God so that all nations might believe and obey him.
—Romans 16:25-26

Sage and I walk the wooded trail by the creek which flows near our little home. We meander slowly along this familiar dirt path, relishing the quiet of the October dawn with its crisp air and tranquil blue and peach sky. Although my springer's eyes do not see where we are going, she has traveled this trail numerous times in the three years since she came to live at our rental house. The crystalline creek and this peaceful pathway are two primary reasons my husband and I chose this place. When the vet diagnosed Sage with Progressive Retinal Atrophy (PRA) and explained to us she would become blind, we began to traverse this trail frequently, so that Sage's mind could more easily comprehend the area and become extremely familiar with the bends in the path. Our vet explained that if we repeated routes frequently, her cognitive mapping would, like a navigation system in a car, recall the twists and turns, the layout of the land so to speak, so that when she completely lost her sight, outings would be easier for her.

We walk; Sage sniffs and I observe and listen. Chickadees twitter in the early morning light, and robins which had yet to navigate south, hop on the ground looking for their breakfast. As a springer spaniel, Sage's sense of smell dominates much of her outdoor experience, and we stop frequently so she can take in the various fragrances which permeate the woodland. I often wonder, without the ability to see, how much more of a mystery the world must be for Sage. I take vision for granted, and I am quite thankful I still have visual perception as a strong sense. Yet, Sage's ability to experience her world without sight, her willingness to investigate both outdoors and indoors via her other senses captivates me; those other senses must be incredibly strong. I wonder what a chickadee smells like. I marvel at the mystery of how olfactory glands work, especially in a hunting breed such as a springer.

A pile of vegetation distracts Sage. At least that's what it is to me, simply a large mound of yellow and brown cotton-wood leaves mingled with a batch of smaller willow wander-ings. Her black muzzle nudges the foliage then forges deeper into the pile. She begins pawing at it, lifting several of the lightweight sheets of nature's compost from the ground. Her digging becomes more intense, and soon the pile succumbs to the plowing paw and parts like the Red Sea. I pull back on Sage's leash, uncertain as to what might be hiding in that wafting covering. Just as I take a few steps closer, out scur-ries a vole, larger than a mouse but smaller than a ground squirrel, most likely planning his autumn home near the creek. Sage's nose stays to the ground as she tracks the little creature toward the grove of willows. I let her take several hastening steps, but pull back tightly on the leash.

"Let's let that one go, girl—this is its home, and we have a walk to finish."

As we continue our walk, Sage finds evidences of other

animals, including mule deer tracks, a Blue Jay feather, and black bear scat. The latter stops me for several minutes, for though I had been told black bears occasionally moseyed along the creek when food became scarce in the mountains, I have never seen such blatant evidence this close to our home. Studying the contents—mostly chokecherries—I marvel at the fact I could live in town and have bears almost in my backyard. Foraging, sleeping, walking, so many incredible, secretive creatures living in our nearby woods. Intriguing to Sage though she can't see them, and also to me, who occasionally gets glimpses.

In much the same way, God is a mystery—he is beyond human comprehension. From the workings of the human body to the creativeness of nature, from his all-encompassing forgiveness to his immeasurable love, God is vast and unexplainable. Job 11:7-8 says, "Do you think you can explain the mystery of God? Do you think you can diagram God Almighty? God is far higher than you can imagine, far deeper than you can comprehend" (THE MESSAGE). Part of the beauty of faith is mystery. Many people want to believe only in things they can see, things that can be explained. How grateful I am for faith in those things I cannot see and for the fact I don't have to know and explain everything. Even Solomon, considered the wisest king to ever live, says, "Just as you'll never understand the mystery of life forming in a pregnant woman, so you'll never understand the mystery at work in all that God does" (Ecclesiastes 11:5, THE MESSAGE).

Although I cannot see God, I do experience evidence of him. From the striking sunrises and sunsets, to the vast landscapes and diverse creatures, creation whispers and sometimes loudly proclaims the majesty and mystery of the Creator. David saw and marveled at the Lord in creation. He writes, "The heavens declare the glory of God; the skies proclaim the work of his hands" (Psalm 19:1). So many things in creation are shrouded in mystery. Why do deer shed antlers and bison don't shed horns? Why are some trees always green and others lose their leaves? Why do cats tend to be loners but dogs are so social? Why do the planets vary so, and the Earth is the only one inhabitable (so far)? There is too much to fathom in this mega-tropolis universe!

God's enigmatic ways prevalent in nature cause many humans great alarm and uncertainty. People often wonder why a good God would allow bad things to happen. From unspeakable violence to incredible natural disasters, many people shake their heads and say they cannot believe in a God who allows such terrible tragedies to occur. Yet, one word tells the why: fall. Humankind fell from grace and fellowship with God when Adam and Eve disobeyed God's instructions. People today continue disobeying God; and it's only through his grace and the acceptance of his Son that a relationship with God the Father can be restored.

Creation, including people, need restoration and liberty; and only after God reveals his glory (see Romans 8:18-23) will God reveal his mysteries. Isaiah records, "'For my thoughts are not your thoughts, neither are your ways my ways,' declares the Lord" (Isaiah 55:8). I cannot fully comprehend God's ways now, but one day all that is hidden will be made known. I accept by faith the many mysteries of the Creator.

Those mysteries are amazing! The mystery of creation, the mystery of grace and redemption, the mysteries of his divine truth—all remarkably beautiful and aligned with hope! From Creation and the Ten Commandments to the Virgin Birth and the message of the Gospel, I find faith and peace. Just as Sage enjoyed exploring the mysteries of those things she could not see, so I enjoy exploring the mysterious ways of my Lord. His grace may be mysterious, yet it's not unreachable. His love is a mystery, yet it's not unattainable.

Just as Jesus stretched out his arms on a cross and paid the price for my sin, so does my heavenly Father open his arms to embrace me with mercy. All I need to do is open my hands to receive this mysterious gift of grace and love.

As Isaiah says, God's ways are not the same as human ways—his love is so much deeper and his forgiveness so much greater! The Apostle Paul declares that God's love is endless and is beyond comprehension (see Ephesians 3:18-19). God is a mystery that, unlike most novels, is not dark and gloomy. Instead, his is a story laced with love and brimming with benevolence.

Many mysteries are wrapped with pleasant surprises. A rainbow after a storm, a lost pet returning home, the constellations of planets and stars.... Even Old Testament prophets experienced positive surprises. Ezekiel records, "Then he took me back to the riverbank. While sitting on the bank, I noticed a lot of trees on both sides of the river. He told me, 'This water flows east, descends to the Arabah and then into the sea, the sea of stagnant waters. When it empties into those waters, the sea will become fresh. Wherever the river flows, life will flourish ... because the river is turning the salt sea into fresh water'" (Ezekiel 47:7-9, THE MESSAGE). God's creativity and power were displayed to Ezekiel and have been shown to numerous others. Consider the parting of the Red Sea when the Israelites left Egypt and were pursued by Pharaoh (see Exodus 14:15) and the raising of Lazarus from the dead (see John 11:40-44). God's love and majesty are incredible mysteries. His grace-filled, unmerited favor is a pleasant, joyous surprise! Though God can be a mystery and beyond my comprehension, I don't have to fully understand everything he is and all that he does to know who he is and that I can place my faith in him. Faith, like God, is a mystery, and one day all that has been hidden, but that has been accepted in trust and faith, will be revealed.

God doesn't want to remain a complete mystery to people, though. He created humankind in his own image, and he wants us to know him. "You will seek me and find me when you seek me with all your heart," God told Jeremiah in chapter 29 verse 13. Mysteries begin to be revealed when one seeks the Lord fully, as Daniel discovered: "During the night the mystery was revealed to Daniel in a vision. Then [he] praised the God of heaven" (Daniel 2:19). Daniel was diligent in seeking answers and he tirelessly sought God for knowledge and understanding. God encourages me to follow Daniel's example to discover the Lord and to discern what he shows. He promises to reveal himself when I tenaciously, honestly seek him, even if I do not completely comprehend what I am seeking.

Sage sought things by digging and smelling. She searched in dirt and in snow. She was diligent in her quest to learn what was hidden. Just as my blind dog eagerly explored the world using the senses she still possessed, I can eagerly engage my senses to discover and better know my Creator God. When I seek to know him, the shadow of mystery slowly fades, as fog evaporates from a mirror. And though I cannot know fully until the day Jesus returns and reveals himself completely, I can begin to detect and discern as I anticipate the mystery of knowing and being fully known:

> *Now we see but a poor reflection as in a mirror; then we shall see face to face. Now I know in part; then I shall know fully, even as I am fully known* (1 Corinthians 13:12).

PRAYER:
Heavenly Father, thank you for your mysterious ways and for your love and your grace. Thank you for the beauty of your creation. Thank you that even though I do not know or understand everything, I can be confident that you do. May I grow in faith, trusting you in the mystery of who you are. Amen.

"Hello, are you friend or foe?"
Sniffing the strange animal across the back fence

Listening to the melodies of creation near Yellowstone National Park

7
Friendship

"The righteous choose their friends carefully." –Proverbs 12:26

Our campsite at the base of the Lower Bighorn Mountains is peaceful. Only three sites are available at this remote location, and on this midsummer Saturday evening, the other two remain unoccupied. Greg and I are taking an excursion to see the beauty of this place we've only heard about until now. It's our first outdoor camping trip with Sage. I finish washing the dishes from a picnic of hamburgers and salad, while Greg goes to the car to start pulling out everything he needs for putting up the tent. Our car is only a few months old, purchased when I started a new job. It is a 2003 Toyota Matrix and the hatchback is great for hauling camp gear and a forty-five-pound English springer spaniel.

I dry my hands on a towel and look over at Sage who is picketed to the picnic table with a long red lead. She is lying underneath the table, head on her paws, listening to my movements. I clap my hands and call her name, then approach as she raises her head. I unhook her from the tether and fasten a leash to her collar. I coax her out, and we take a walk along the road that leads to the campground.

The Bighorn Mountains rise seven- to nine-thousand feet

and several of the peaks are within view of the camping area. Sage and I slowly walk, her ears listening and her nose smelling, while my eyes behold the majesty around me. Rocky cliffs jet out from some of the peaks, while the lower meadows resonate in shades of red and green. Much of Wyoming is dry plains, but such high country as this has moisture from snowmelt. A narrow, clear creek meanders near the campground. The streambed boasts large boulders, between which nestle yellow columbine, purple lupine, and white daisies. Visiting this area for the first time, I am amazed at the vibrancy and awed by the tranquility. I sit on a big rock and simply bask in the solitude and splendor.

Sage, muzzle high in the air, takes a deep sniff, as if drinking from the clear stream. She remains still for several moments. Quiet companionship envelopes us as I rest my hand on her head. I scratch her ears and feast my eyes on the peaceful scene.

About twenty minutes later we return to the campsite where my husband is sitting on a canvas folding chair near the fire pit. A small yet warm fire blazes near his feet. He, too, is looking at the scenery; he smiles when Sage and I return.

"Have a nice walk?" he asks.

"Very nice. Sure is peaceful and lovely here."

He agrees. Then he tells me, "I forgot the tent stakes."

"What?!"

"We'll have to sleep in the car tonight."

I look at our little blue hatchback and wonder if two people and a forty-five-pound dog can all fit comfortably for a full night. But somehow the Matrix proves just large enough for all three of us, although it isn't easy or terribly restful. Greg and I lie in our sleeping bags on the air mattress and Sage finds a comfortable spot between us. We feel warm and snug together. But turning over is not an option, and between my husband's and my dog's snores, little sleep comes to me. The things friends endure for each other!

Greg and I had spent several months looking for the right dog to add to our home, and I believe we chose well. Sage and I shared many incredible experiences during our time together, from camping trips to road trips; from walking wooded forest lands to strolls in our neighborhood; from visiting schools and libraries to curling up by the woodstove and sitting in my recliner; from weekends visiting my parents' Montana cabin to emergency treks to the vet's office; from exciting and tense to laid back and stress free. We bonded closely and experienced some of the greatest joys and deepest fears and sorrows together. I happily say that Sage was my friend and I was hers!

Friends are truly special gifts from God. Most times those friends are human, but not always. Pets have nearly always been part of my life, and I've considered those animals my friends.

Thankfully, I also have human friends! I remain friends with several women from my childhood days in Iowa—people I don't see often, but still talk with on the phone and communicate with via letters, and that ultimate techno communication system, Facebook! I have friends and acquaintances at church, in my neighborhood, in various states, and even around the world. People at work are friends, and people with whom I have things in common are friends. My husband is my friend, my mother is my best friend, and my pets are my dear friends. Friendships are valuable, and friendships are vital to one's existence.

Jesus understood the importance of friendship. He tells his disciples in John 15:15, "I no longer call you servants, because a servant does not know his master's business. Instead, I have called you friends, for everything that I learned from my Father I have made known to you." Twelve men shared Jesus' life and ministry for three years. They traveled with him, ate with him, listened to him, and heard him say, "Greater love has no one than this: to lay down one's life for one's friends" (John 15:13). All but one of the twelve disciples carried on his work after Jesus' death and ascension to the Father, and they gave their life for his name's sake, remembering his words. When I follow Christ closely, taking the time to know him, I discover the treasure of his loving friendship, the friend who laid his life down for me, whose companionship is eternal.

Soldiers in foxholes understand this concept. Millions of men have died in battle not only for their country, but also for their comrades. Dogs have given their lives for their human families—even for strangers at times: from bomb-sniffing dogs and K-9 units to a family pet that rescues a drowning swimmer.

Sage was not a hero in the sense that she had given her life for me or protected me from an unknown assailant. But her companionship and her attitude of overcoming challenges endeared me to her.

I wrote and published a children's book about Sage in 2007. The first library Sage and I visited that summer was in West Yellowstone, Montana, the community where I served as newspaper editor during the mid '90s. A small community tucked on the western edge of Yellowstone National Park, the summer boasts not only thousands of tourists, but also a quaint community library with a children's program. I wanted to read *Sage's Big Adventure* to the children there, because this place carries special memories for me. After I shared some of Sage's adventures with blindness, the children had the opportunity to meet her face-to-face. Amidst all the pats, hugs and kisses, a six-year-old girl with her arms around Sage's neck, said, "I love you!" Sage responded with a happy lick to her cheek.

Children and dogs belong together like ice cream and chocolate sauce. A dog can touch a child who is hurting and lonely and needs a friend. A dog can also impact the elderly in nursing homes and cancer-stricken adults in a hospital. No wonder the saying goes, "Dogs are man's best friends."

During the first few years Sage lived with us, we frequently visited my parents' cabin in central Montana. Here, five miles from the nearest paved road, we spent weekends walking the cactus-infested Missouri River Breaks region. I often had to pull painful cactus quills from my shoes and from Sage's paws. Yet, this did not deter us from enjoying the sounds and smells of the outdoors. Whether on or off leash, Sage enjoyed wandering, sniffing, and listening as well as lying under a bulging Ponderosa pine or on the wooden front porch of the cabin.

Springers are hunting dogs, and Sage's instincts kicked in during these excursions. She would lift her front leg in a pointer stance and her bushy tail would stand erect as she "found" songbirds, ladybugs, or rabbits with her incredible ears and amazing nose.

On this earth I have both two-legged and four-legged friends. There are the two-legged kind who enjoy the companionship of the four-legged kind, and we share stories and concerns about our pets. Then there are those with whom I have a Christian connection, ones with whom I have a college connection, and ones with whom I share a childhood connection. There are others with whom I have a connection to creation, enjoying hikes or strolls through forests and fields of flowers. Sage and I shared such a connection, and we enjoyed those things so much, that Greg and I purchased a mountain property and cabin where we strolled through pine forests, encountering robins and rabbits, deer and dragonflies, savoring the moments of exploration and relaxation.

I still smile at the memory of that camping trip with Sage when we all slept in the car. It was a pleasant, though not terribly comfortable, time shared with friends. We were thankful for the empty campsites next to us, so there was no one to witness our fiasco!

PRAYER:

Thank you, Lord, for my many friends. Whether they are people or pets, they are all a gift from you. Thank you also for your amazing, loving, sacrificial friendship. Help me to always be the best friend I can be, to those on this earth and to you.

"Our happy family"
Gayle and Greg Irwin with Cody and Sage at their mountain cabin

8

Confidence

I am still confident of this: I will see the goodness of the LORD in the land of the living. –Psalm 27:13

My senses fill with the abundance of nature around me on this April day—the cattails wobbling in the breeze, the contrasting scents of lily flowers in the pond and deer pellets in the dirt. Sage and I are enjoying a quiet walk along the dirt trail that surrounds the marsh in Ocean Lake Wildlife Habitat Management Area in Wyoming.

Two years blind now, Sage lowers her head, her keen black nose snuffling the pathway, seeking each fragrance. Her sensitive ears perk up intently for each sound. We hear meadowlarks sing clear and sweet in the grass stalks and yellow-headed blackbirds scold from the cattails.

Spaniels are bred and often trained to hunt birds; my black-and-white five-year-old girl is in her element. With her lack of sight, she may not be the avid bird hunter that her ancestors were, but she still relishes the sounds and smells of the multitude of birds we encounter throughout the day. Her confidence is not diminished. She walks with the same poise as a sighted springer during a pheasant hunt. In fact, on occasion, her right front leg cocks in a pointing stance, reflecting her regal breed. I smile and praise her, patting her side gently, as that leg and tail remain on point for several minutes. We slowly walk on, relishing the time spent in nature amidst God's creation.

Then, with ears erect, Sage perks up her head when a new bird sound echoes across the landscape. It is the sound I was hoping to hear today: the amazing call of a sandhill crane. I watch as two of these graceful reddish-gray birds with red foreheads take flight, their impressive six-foot wing span displayed just one-hundred yards in front of us.

Sage's head tilts in the direction of the "caw-caw" sound.

"Those are the birds I told you about, Sage. They are incredible!"

I've seen sandhill cranes in each state in which I've lived, from Wisconsin to Idaho. Standing five feet tall with gangly black legs and long black bills, a few of them migrate each spring through the central part of Wyoming on their way to northern and western summer sites. Though I know Sage can't see these magnificent birds nor fully understand what I told her, she seems to enjoy the new sound of this unknown creature, as well as other delights of sounds and smells of this new location.

Sage didn't always display such confidence and poise, especially when we encountered other dogs during our daily trail walks or in the dog park. When an unleashed dog would run up to greet her, Sage cowered and struggled to get as close to me as possible. Sometimes she growled and bared her teeth. I eventually came to realize that because she could not see the body language of the other dog, she took the defensive or submissive role; most dogs relate to each other with posturing and watch for the other dog's stance. But since she did not know whether the approaching dog was friend or foe, she assumed the worst. I learned not to walk her in areas where we would encounter other dogs, or walk early enough in the morning to avoid those situations. If we did encounter another dog, I kept Sage close to me or put myself between Sage and the other dog to protect her from not only possible danger, but also from her fear of an encounter. When I explained to people walking their dog near us that Sage was blind, they often politely let us pass or went around us and kept their dog in check. Sage's confidence waned during encounters with other dogs. She was more secure, however, when she pressed against me; she knew that I was there to help and to defend her.

Similarly, I am reassured when I remember who I am in Christ. The knowledge that I am God's beloved gives me greater confidence as I face life's uncertainties. John, Jesus' beloved disciple, writes, "How great is the love the Father has lavished on us, that we should be called children of God! And that is what we are!" (1 John 3:1). Yet, it is not a cocky confidence. Although I am a child of the Most High God, I am also called to be humble. Isaiah 66:2 says that God esteems those who are humble and contrite in spirit, and who tremble at his Word.

When we recognize that all good gifts come from God (see James 1:17) we can also acknowledge that our strengths and abilities do not come from our own selves, but from a gracious God.

Despite the darkness and many uncertainties, Sage moved through most situations of life with great confidence. She entered classrooms and libraries with numerous strangers' voices, and she rarely cowered. She may have stood near me for reassurance, but she didn't seek to hide nor did she cringe in fear. She allowed people to pet her and little children to hug her. One might expect a dog with her disability to shrink from a stranger's voice and touch. But Sage's trust in me gave her confidence in herself. By the same token, my trust in the Lord gives me self-confidence. "Blessed is the man who trusts in the LORD, whose confidence is in him," says Jeremiah 17:7.

If I am truly God's child and the blood of Christ covers me, then why are there times when I don't live confidently as God's beloved? I question myself. I question God. I doubt myself. I doubt God. I waver and waft, wondering about decisions, worrying about life. When I do all that, I end up weaving a web of chaos.

When I think of Sage, who confidently wagged her tail and walked on sidewalks and stairs that she could not see, I often wonder why my own faith is sometimes still so small. When I trust in the Lord and am confident in who he is and what he does, I gain both confidence and peace. "The fruit of righteousness will be peace," Isaiah writes. "The effect of righteousness will be quietness and confidence forever" (Isaiah 32:17).

Sage enjoyed sleeping on dog beds. Wherever a blanket or rug was spread, she would lie on it. She would even attempt to curl up in a much smaller cat bed. The first time I saw her do that, I laughed aloud. Imagine a fifty-five pound English springer spaniel curling up in an oval-shaped fuzzy twelve-inch cat bed! I wonder if she forgot she was a medium-sized dog, and not a small cat!

Sometimes I, too, forget who I am. As a younger woman, when my romantic relationships ended and my heart felt forever broken, my self esteem was shot. Despite the fact that I had put myself through college, completed a degree, and was on a career path, I found myself at a crossroad. For months I wandered through the maze of my mind, wondering, "Where do I go from here?" Thankfully, through a spiritual retreat I attended during my mid-thirties, I once again met my Creator, who reminded me I belonged to him, and that as long as I put my trust in him, I don't have to feel lost or lack confidence. I don't have to try to squeeze myself into someone else's mold as Sage squeezed herself into a tiny cat bed.

There are still times when my confidence is challenged. Like most people, I juggle various responsibilities and sometimes question whether I have strength to handle those responsibilities, or the ability to complete certain tasks. When doubt comes, I need only turn to God's Word and discover such positive truths as: "I can do everything through him who gives me strength" (Philippians 4:13) and "Being confident of this, that he who began a good work in you will carry it on to completion until the day of Christ Jesus" (Philippians 1:6).

Confidence in Christ is my motto. What I can do through Christ, in the will of God, helps me climb new heights and scale large walls. Adapting to life with a blind dog is not necessarily an easy task. My husband and I had to adjust our lives to some degree. We lived in the same house for nearly six years and very rarely rearranged furniture. When we moved into a new home, we worked with Sage to help her understand the new arrangements. We had to be vigilant about pushing dining chairs close to the table and not leave things lying around the house that could trip her or inadvertently cause her harm. Even the yard needed to be as safe for Sage as it would be for a toddler; we trimmed bushes consistently so that protruding twigs would not stab her. We hung chimes from the patio corner and taught her various commands to help her navigate. Sage's confidence matured so that she was able to leap upon a queen-sized bed she couldn't see and easily travel up and down the stairs.

Because of our experience and our initial concerns about having a blind dog, I envisioned others who received the news their dog was going blind would have similar concerns and questions about their ability as well as the quality of life for their dog. Those thoughts prompted me to put together an e-book called *Help! My Dog is Going Blind!* which provides anecdotes from my experience with Sage and offers tips and encouragement on how owners of blind dogs can better help themselves and their pets adjust to the disability. God used Sage—and our life together—and the confidence we both gained through our experiences to encourage others and give them greater confidence to face the challenge of blindness in their beloved pets.

Confidence is often matured through challenge and strengthened through trust. If I was nearby when Sage stumbled or bumped into something, I reached out to help her. Similarly, when I fall or make a mistake and ask for God's help, he responds. "This is the confidence we have in approaching God: that if we ask anything according to his will, he hears us," says 1 John 5:14. When I tremble in fear and doubt, I seek God's guidance and assistance. I am reassured by his Word and by his previous work in my life that he cares and that he listens.

People place their confidence in many things, from the kitchen chair they sit on to the airplane they board for travel. People put their confidence in banks, bonds, and borders, yet those banks can be robbed, bond prices sink, and borders invaded. Paul notes that I should put no confidence in the flesh (see Philippians 3:3). Instead, I am to have confidence in a sovereignty I cannot see. When I trust his plan, he will be my confidence and will not let me stumble.

Just as Sage grew in confidence through the years, so, too, have I. Knowing I can approach the throne of God because I am his beloved child and recognizing that I can rely upon him to strengthen and sustain me gives me greater confidence. "Such confidence as this is ours through Christ before God. Not that we are competent in ourselves to claim anything for ourselves, but our competence comes from God" (2 Corinthians 3:4-5). That confidence grows as I seek to learn about God and to rely upon him, just as Sage relied upon me. I have experienced a strengthening of my confidence because of the maturing of my faith in my caregiver—God. When I focus my belief in him and his plan, he provides me with greater confidence to accomplish those things he wants me to do and to become the person he wants me to be.

PRAYER:
Lord, help me to recognize and honor who I am in Christ, and to grow in faith and confidence in you and in myself. Help me to seek your plan and know your will so that I can mature in my walk with you. Amen.

9
Joy

*Surely you have granted him unending blessings and made him
glad with the joy of your presence. –Psalm 21:6*

On the living room floor I sit next to Sage brushing her
wispy black-and-white coat. Grooming is an activity we
conduct weekly. Sage's fine fur is easy to bathe and brush,
and she enjoys not only the process, but also the companionship we share during these experiences. Sage is a joyful dog.
She rolls, wiggles, wags and woofs frequently. I often marvel
that a dog with such significant disabilities can be so happy.
Perhaps this is because of her unique personality, and also
because of how comfortable and secure she is with our love
and in our home.

Springers are generally happy dogs. Though the
Springer Spaniel is an active breed, Sage's disability keeps
her mostly quiet and calm. Yet, often her delight is obvious: leaping into the air and sounding off whenever a
squirrel captures her attention; snuffling along the trail
during forested walks, tail waving high in anticipation of
woodland smells; generous barks of welcome when Greg
or I return home after a day at work. All of these bring
Sage great pleasure, and she exhibits her joy in numerous

ways. Even the pull of a brush across her fine coat gives her delight. In addition to sitting still for the weekly manicure, Sage lies calmly on her side and even turns herself belly up for soft strokes to her stomach—which she gets this day.

I run the grooming brush gently down her back, over her head, and across her sides. Sage sits quietly, luxuriating in the light strokes to her fur and skin. I push her firmly but gently to a "down" position, repeat the combing process, then she vulnerably turns more onto her back, exposing her belly for more ministrations. I then tickle and massage that white and pink exposure. Sage wiggles her body back and forth. She sneezes then snorts her pleasure, and the shimmying begins again. I laugh. When a dog rolls around or wags its tail, it is displaying pure joy, and Sage, despite her disability, is no exception to this canine rule of behavior!

I set the grooming tools aide, but Sage doesn't want the session to end. She again rolls over onto her back for another tummy rub, and I oblige. She wriggles her body from side to side, sashaying her back end, nose pointed heavenward and snorting with pleasure. For a dog to take such a vulnerable position, belly upward, displays complete trust and submission.

As I sit next to Sage, rubbing her tummy and caressing her chin, I ask myself: *How often do I show my vulnerable side to others I love, even to God? Do I display or voice delight in the care and attention that God gives to me?*

While people show their joy in myriads of ways—laughter, artistic expression, singing, dancing, and praising—dogs have their own canine ways of expressing joy. Before Sage lost her hearing at age eleven, I simply needed to say her name softly and her tail would thump vigorously against the floor. If I snapped the metal clip of her leash several times, indicating a walk, that tail wagged even harder because she had learned what that snapping sound meant. When I would come home from somewhere, even if I had only been gone for thirty minutes, Sage's tail would beat enthusiastically when she realized I was home. She sometimes bayed song-like, *Awhoo, awhoo.* I received either a touch from her paw or a sniff by her spaniel nose, and then I rubbed behind her ears, petted her cheeks, and scratched under her chin. And, of course, she loved to get belly rubs! Her joy at my return was obvious. That contagious joy would bring a smile to my face.

The joy that Sage exhibited upon my return home was not unlike the story of the prodigal son. Found in Luke chapter fifteen, this tale of forgiveness is also a story of joy. The boy may have squandered his inheritance; he may have been an arrogant, demanding child; and he may have made some poor choices. But when the boy returned home, his father's love and elation were apparent. When he was still a long way off, his father saw him and was filled with compassion for him; he ran to his son, threw his arms around him and kissed him.

The father delighted at his son's return. I'm sure he shouted the boy's name and cried tears of ecstasy. When I travel apart from my Heavenly Father and seek to return, deep in my spirit I can hear him call my name, joyfully welcoming me back into his loving embrace. Just as Sage's joy upon my return was contagious, the Father's joy at my return makes me smile because I know I'm accepted, forgiven and loved. I delight in his presence much like Sage delighted in my presence. I know his love and merciful grace abound.

I experience joy when I witness a crimson sunset or an apricot sunrise; I experience joy when my husband walks in the door with flowers for no apparent reason; I experience joy when my supervisor praises me for something accomplished at work; I experience joy when a friend I haven't seen in several years arranges a "girls time" mid way between our cities; I also experienced joy when my blind dog shimmied to me and licked my face ... or even when she was soundly sleeping at my feet, cuddling as close as she could get. When I was a college student, I enjoyed going dancing—the music and movement filled me with joy. The first time I saw the ocean and the massive gray whales that make their home in the deep blue sea, I was awestruck and ecstatic. There are so many positive pleasures in life! The greatest joy I experience, however, is when I remember the price my Savior paid for me to spend eternity in heaven, and that the final chapter of my life on earth is the beginning of my life story in heaven.

Joy should be the mark of a Christian. The Apostle Paul instructs in I Thessalonians 5:16-18, "Be joyful always; pray continually; and give thanks in all circumstances for this is God's will for you in Christ Jesus." Is that really possible? Truthfully, I find that command extremely challenging, especially in the midst of discouragements and setbacks. Perhaps I live more in my flesh than I do in the Spirit. Perhaps I try too hard in my own strength instead of relying on God's strength. This is still an area of struggle for me.

Most people experience trials and challenges in life. Some endure greater problems than others, yet whatever the tragedy, it is personal and heartfelt. I have known people who have suddenly lost children and spouses to accidents; others have experienced major health issues.

First hand I have witnessed people who exhibit joy despite cancer, despite broken hearts, and despite financial tsunamis. Witnessing a positive response in someone else in spite of their difficult circumstances is such an encouragement to me when I face trials of my own.

A few years back, I experienced one of the most difficult

trials of my life. I received the call that my father had experienced a light stroke. The emergency room doctor of the Montana hospital found a problem with his heart and it was decided that he needed surgery. I was staying the night with my mother when at 1:30 a.m. I awoke to the sound of her weakened voice calling to me from the bathroom. I was not prepared for what I found. My mother was covered in blood coming from her mouth like a geyser erupting. She couldn't control the flow, and I couldn't stop it. I dialed 9-1-1. Within minutes, the volunteer ambulance crew arrived and whisked her to the hospital forty miles away.

While my father was down the hall recovering, my mother arrived at the emergency room. During that time of uncertainty I was not necessarily joyful in my circumstance, but I was joyful in the Lord as I reminisced about the wonderful life I had shared with my mom and dad—the vacations, the laughter, the security and love they provided. Thankfully, they each recovered. I still have more time with both of my parents. I don't know how much time, but I try not to waste it. I call and visit them as frequently as I can.

If I had lost my mother or father during that time, would I still be able to count that as joy? Yes, I believe so, because both parents have a firm faith in God; and I know that death is a part of life and there is life after this earthly journey. Would I have rejoiced in the circumstance of my parents' death? Have I rejoiced in the circumstance of other family or friends' deaths? No, not in the circumstance, but I rejoice in God. I am blessed to still have my parents in my life. But when the Lord does call them home, I will have to release them into God's presence. I will grieve but be joyful in my memories of our time together, of the love and support they've given me, and the many answered prayers we've experienced as a family.

Sage's joy was also her strength. When setbacks

occurred, such as walking into walls, stumbling on steps, or going deaf, Sage didn't let joy disappear for more than a few moments or a few days. Her delight in life and in her companionship with Greg and me was fully apparent when her tail wagged, when she wiggled and rolled on the floor, and when her voice resounded with *Awhoo! Awhoo!* throughout the house. Sage epitomized the words of the hymn: "Joyful, joyful, we adore thee, God of glory, LORD of love."

PRAYER:
Lord, may my life more greatly reflect joy, mirroring the strength you provide despite my circumstances. May I share that joy with others through encouragement and understanding. And may I be more adoring toward you, the provider of all my blessings.

10
Compassion

But you, LORD, are a compassionate and gracious God, slow to anger, abounding in love and faithfulness.
—Psalm 86:15

Two weeks have passed since my parents were hospitalized within twenty-four hours of each other. I am able to stay at their house and help care for them while they are recovering. My husband has driven back home after a brief visit but has left Sage with us.

As Mom naps, I relax in the recliner to read a book. My dad is restless. He wanders the rooms of the house then goes outside. Through the picture window I see him pacing the front yard. When he comes back in, Sage raises her head from the doggie bed on the living-room floor. She stands up and walks over to greet him. He pats her head absently then sits in his chair, staring into space. I watch from the corner of my eye as Sage carefully finds her way to him and sits beside his chair. She reaches up a paw and pats his leg. Dad reaches down and strokes her head. Sage scoots as close to his chair as she can get, wedging herself between his legs. Both of Dad's hands are now petting her, for she insists on it. A peaceful look comes over Dad's face.

I am reminded of studies reporting that people relax physically and emotionally from the simple act of petting a dog or cat. I smile with pride, watching my disabled dog dishing out therapy to my distressed father.

Sage seemed to have a special sense for those in need, to understand when someone was sad or scared. She appeared to comprehend a person's anxiety or loneliness. When I experienced those feelings or when I was ill, Sage would seek me out and insist on staying close to me. Many dogs are trained as therapy animals, providing comfort to those confined to hospital beds and nursing homes. Sage had no such training, yet she seemed to have inherited this sixth sense, knowing when a person needed the calming effect of her subtle, comforting company. When we visited various classrooms, for example, Sage often sought out a child and sat next to him or her for awhile during my presentation. Many times that child would eventually pet Sage or put an arm around her. I would later learn that these particular students were reserved in class or had experienced some type of loss.

Perhaps God provided dogs as a strong reminder of what serving others is all about, maybe even of his own compassion for us. Psalm 145:9 states, "The Lord is good to all. He has compassion on all he has made." I've experienced God's compassion in my own life and in the lives of people I know. God displayed his compassion upon a friend who was battling cancer; Greg and I gathered with her, other friends and her family to pray for her before a surgery, and when the surgeons began the operation a few days later, they found no cancer in her body! Another friend has a young son that was diagnosed with leukemia, and he has been in remission for several years now. Although I haven't personally battled such significant health issues, God has answered my prayers for protection, both while traveling the highways of this land and while visiting locations away from home. What a comfort to know God cares!

The book of Matthew records many instances of Jesus showing compassion for people. From those who were physically sick or hungry to those in need of spiritual renewal, Jesus showered his loving care on people. "Jesus went through all the towns and villages, teaching in their synagogues, preaching the good news of the kingdom and healing every disease and sickness. When he saw the crowds, he had compassion, because they were harassed and helpless, like sheep without a shepherd" (Matthew 9:35-36). His compassion always led to action, as he responded to the needs of those around him. He fed the hungry multitudes and offered his healing words and touch to many.

When I see people in trouble, do I show compassion? Do I put myself in their shoes and reach out to help as Jesus did? Compassion is the heart of God, and as his child, I am called to be like him, exhibiting compassion in word and deed. Am I like Christ, or do I just turn my head and heart away and do nothing?

Having a servant's heart is somehow easier when natural disasters strike and when the holiday season rolls around. Monies pour in to assist those who have lost homes to hurricanes and hands pitch in to clean up neighborhoods after an earthquake or tornado. People donate gifts and food to charitable organizations during Thanksgiving and Christmas. I, too, have contributed in these ways, without thinking much about the faces of those who need that assistance … until one Christmas season.

I was late donating toys to the local Salvation Army this particular year and had to drop them off at the distributing warehouse the day families were picking up the contributed items. The line stretched from the front of the building to

nearly outside. People's eyes met mine, and in those eyes
I detected sorrow and in some shame. Tears welled like
a fountain in my eyes and the faces of men and women
coming to receive donated food and toys swam in front of
me. This was my community. These were my neighbors.
God's Spirit pierced my heart by allowing me to witness not
only the number of those in need, but their faces. Never
before had "need" had a face–in this case, hundreds of faces.
And ours was just one small community. I sat in my car and
prayed for God to forgive me for my apathy and selfishness
and to never let me forget those faces.

Every day there are faces of people in need. On television, in magazines and on the Internet pictures of the poor
are displayed. Malnourished children knock at the door of
my heart with their visible ribcages, distended bellies, gaunt
eyes and hollow cheeks. I answered that knock years ago and
began sponsoring children through World Vision. Recently,
the first girl I sponsored graduated from the program with
plans to be a teacher. I wept when I received the news,
just as I wept when I first saw her photo—a bony 9-year-
old, dark-skinned child holding a water bucket. She and
her village benefited from my monthly donation for more
than 10 years, and through the help she received not only
food and water, but also learned about God and received
a formal education, things she may have gone through life
without ever receiving. Her dreams of being a teacher are
being realized, and she will go on to help others in the area. I
am thankful I responded to the Holy Spirit's nudge to show
compassion in this way. I now have a new child to sponsor,
and I am excited to see what changes will come about in
her life because I chose to be Christ-like, to act and not
be apathetic.

God knows I cannot financially help every oppressed
or displaced person. But the one thing I can do when I

see the faces and hear the stories is pray. I pray not only
for the needy, but for those who serve them: the rescue
mission in my community, the people responding to natural
disasters, the missionaries drilling water wells and bringing
the Gospel, the Water of Life, to endless villages. Lifting
their needs and their protection before the throne of mercy
costs nothing but time.

Sage shared her time with others, and she also extended
her concern to other animals. When our cats were still
young kittens, they sometimes cried for their siblings. Sage
searched them out, and when she discovered their location,
she would sit with or lay next to them.

I like to help animals in need when I can: transporting
dogs through the state for rescue groups, helping strays find
their way home, and assisting our local Humane Society
with events and publicity. When I seek God's guidance on
how best to share my time and treasures with those in
need, both people and pets, the Holy Spirit leads, because
compassion is the character of Christ.

One way I try to follow Christ's example is to add an
additional sum to certain charities whenever I am blessed
with extra. If God is gracious enough to provide me with
additional funds, the least I can do is donate a small percent-
age for the needy in my community and throughout the
world. I may not be a missionary, but I can help those who
do minister locally and in the far reaches of the world-who
are there to not only share the spiritual food of God, but also
to feed starving stomachs, offer an education, drill a water
well, or help plant a field.

The apostle James instructs God's people to look after
orphans and widows (see James 1:27). Many organizations
have heeded the call to help care for the poor, the widows
and the orphans. Throughout the world, groups such as
Compassion International, World Vision, and Samaritan's

Purse respond to crises of war, famine and disaster throughout the world. These volunteers and staff help families by providing clean water and teaching trades. Stomachs are filled and spirits are renewed as they are shown the love of Jesus and are treated with compassion. Hundreds of thousands of lives are positively impacted. I can be and am part of that influence. I gave up driving through the local coffee vendors three times a week in order to take on an additional child sponsorship. I make my own specialty coffee at home more often now, plus I save myself some time! When I receive a letter or a progress report, noting how well the girls are doing in school and how positively the villages are affected, I thank the Lord for his provision to me through which I can bless others.

"Blessed is he who has regard for the weak," David writes in Psalm 41:1. Sage possessed the ability to note a person's weakness. In spite of her own weakness, she offered a willing paw and a comforting presence to the downcast. My heavenly Father had such tremendous compassion that he willingly sent Jesus to this earth to display that empathy in acts of mercy. But, no greater concern was shown than through Jesus' death on my behalf. If God showed such compassion for me, how can I remain indifferent to the plight of others?

PRAYER:
"Lord, forgive my apathy; help me to put faces to those in need. Give me a more compassionate heart toward the poor and oppressed of this world. As you were and are compassionate towards me, help me be more concerned and caring towards others. Amen."

Sage with one of her many friends

"Where'd that treat go?"
Sage mastering a new set of stairs

11
Humility

*If my people, who are called by my name, will humble themselves
and pray and seek my face and turn from their wicked ways, then
I will hear from heaven and will forgive their sin and will heal
their land.* −2 *Chronicles 7:14*

A turquoise sky welcomes us to Idaho. It is the height of
summer. I park the car on the gravel lot, and Greg and I, Sage
and my parents step from the vehicle. We gaze upon a prairie
that stretches for miles until snow-capped mountains break
the horizon. Approaching the log-sided visitor's center, we are
welcomed by the manager, Laura. I met Laura a few months
ago when she agreed to host a presentation featuring Sage and
me. Her own dog, a short-haired, bi-colored dachshund, is
also disabled; and she thought sharing our experiences would
offer a great family presentation.

Upon entering the building, we are greeted by a barrage
of barking. Lovie, the doxie, races toward us, motoring with
the velocity of an Indy 500 driver. Back legs paralyzed, she
is assisted by a little K-9 cart, a two-wheeled contraption
attached to her back end. As Greg, my parents and the two
dogs return to the beauty of the outside, Laura and I set up
one table with photos of our dogs and also my books, and

a second table for my computer by which I will conduct a Powerpoint presentation.

As people gather in the room, Laura goes outside to call Lovie. No dachshund. She calls again. Still no Lovie. I step onto the wooden deck that circles the east side of the visitor's center and see Laura walking the perimeter of the building, a young boy following. Laura keeps calling for Lovie, but no wiener dog on wheels appears. Then the boy, about ten years old, shouts, "I see her! She's under the deck!"

Laura and I kneel beside him under the wooden planks. Other people encircle us as we ponder Lovie's plight. Wedged deep under the deck, her little cart's wheels are lodged against a log. Her front legs scramble, attempting to return to her master, but she can't budge. Just moments before, Lovie was jettisoning through and around the center, but now she's stuck.

Laura's young friend responds to the superhero call. The boy elbow-crawls under the deck and frees Lovie from her timber prison. By simply moving the slender log away from the cart's wheels, Lovie is freed. The released dog, finding that the cart's wheels are no longer jammed, dashes toward Laura, wheels whirling behind her. Laura hugs her beloved friend, and the gathered audience laughs with relief.

Back inside the building, where my parents wait with Sage, I bend down and place my arms around my own dog and squeeze her silky-coated body to me. Being stuck, being humble, yet being resilient, are situations she and I understand.

Later, at a picnic site, I looked at my blind dog lying on the blanket with head erect and ears forward. Though her sight was gone, her other senses were in full swing. Her long muzzle stretched upward, taking a deep sniff, and her ears twitched slightly, capturing surrounding sounds. My mind flashed back a few years to the time Sage had gone through two eye surgeries to alleviate pressure building up behind the eyes. Although the operations were months apart, the end result had been total blindness. Glaucoma had set in, just as Dr. Johnson had predicted, but the fluid pressure behind the eyes was painful, so he suggested having the surgery to give her relief from the pain. Since she would be sightless soon even without the operation, Greg and I had agreed to the procedures.

Total blindness impacted Sage like the log impacted Lovie's cart. Although Sage had learned the layout of our house as Lovie had learned the layout of the visitor's center, on occasion Sage would walk into a corner of a room and not know what to do. She couldn't see, so she didn't realize what the obstacle really was, and she didn't recognize that going backwards just a few steps would release her from the obstruction. She was stuck in the corner, just as Lovie was stuck under the porch, and she needed me to guide her out. Lovie, too, needed someone to assist her. I also need guidance in life. But to accept that assistance requires humility.

Humbleness prevails in pets, especially those with special needs. Pets rely upon their owners to take care of them, to feed and provide shelter for them. Special-needs animals, like Sage and Lovie, rely more upon their masters to help them get around, to help them get unstuck.

Although Sage never had a K-9 cart, nor was she ever wedged underneath a wooden deck, she knew what it meant to be stuck. Whether cornered against a wall or lost in the woods, Sage needed assistance to return to her master. She also needed assistance just getting through life. Receiving help is often easier for animals to accept than for people.

Human nature does not readily humble itself and accept assistance. Although I need guidance in my life from my master, God, sometimes I don't ask for that help. Like Lovie,

I race with all wheels spinning. Sometimes I hit my head on a tree, like my blind dog. Other times, like both Lovie and Sage, I get stuck, either by getting myself into a corner or by some unforeseen obstacle. My all-knowing heavenly Father knew exactly what would happen, and yet because I have a free will, he let me motor along. And, like Laura waited for Lovie, my Lord waits for me to humble myself and return to him.

David writes that God "guides the humble in what is right" (see Psalm 25:9). Just as I guided Sage and attempted to keep her from harm, when I humble myself and allow God to guide me, I can be assured he will walk with me and keep me on the right path.

Humility is not weakness. In the book, *Humilitas*, Australian author and pastor John Dickson defines humility as "a willingness to hold power in service of others. Humility does not mean humiliation … Nor does it mean being a doormat for others." Lowering oneself, redirecting one's power in service of others, is the positive, true sense of humility. That is how Jesus lived and how he died. His humbleness led to his death, which leads to my eternal life. Jesus' humility did not make him less of who he was—God's Son. His humility and his certainty also uplift me as I trust and believe in him. Being humble is having confidence in who I am in Christ and to whom I belong. His powerful triumph is humbling and life-altering.

God's awe-inspiring power is also evident in the natural world. While we spent time in the forest after the visitor's center presentation, my family and I ate our lunch and walked around the colorful, remote area. Sage sniffed at trees and flowers and rooted in the dirt with her nose. But on occasion she paused, sat in the midst of that flowering meadow and simply listened. I, too, basked in the serenity and majesty of the moment, awed by the marvels of God's amazing creation.

We were on the fringe of Yellowstone National Park, an

area I worked as a journalist more than a decade before and a place I still visit regularly. Steaming geysers whisper and roar, and crystalline rivers sing a cascading melody. In this region I've encountered bison, bear, elk and other creatures. Each visit to this special landscape provides opportunity to witness God's power and creativity. I discover God in natural grandeur, and that discovery is heart-felt and humbling.

Retreating occasionally from people and pollution opens opportunities to behold the incredible splendor of God. When I look heavenward and experience the infinite universe with its innumerable shimmering stars, I recall Isaiah's declaration, "Lift your eyes and look to the heavens: Who created all these? He who brings out the starry hosts one by one and calls them each by name. Because of his great power and mighty strength, not one of them is missing" (Isaiah 40:26). God makes enough stars to cover an inky sky and beyond, and he cares if one is missing. Therefore, how can I imagine he'd not care about me? When I get stuck in the corner of worry or under the deck of despair, I look at the golden moon as it rises, or the crimson sun as it sets, and I am reminded of God's power and love; I am humbled.

My blind dog usually accepted my leading and commands with humility. But, like most dogs and many people, Sage also could be willful. While on a walk, she sometimes decided she wanted to go in a specific direction and pulled on her leash to go that way. But a tug from me reminded her that I was the guardian and the authority; and she'd relent. Sometimes I, too, let pride get in the way and I attempt to go in a different direction than my Guardian desires. I don't always respond to the tugs God gives. But when I recall the price Jesus paid for me, the caring my heavenly Father has for me, and the power my Lord displays through his beautiful creation, I remember who really is the all-knowing authority. When I am reminded of who he is and whose I am, humbleness wells up like the geysers in Yellowstone.

Just as I led Sage safely and enjoyably (perhaps including a few special sniffs of some new location!), so, too, does my heavenly Father lead me in life. And he lets me enjoy many special moments along the way.

Just as the young boy lifted the log that lodged Lovie under the porch, God lifts me from entanglements. And, just as I coaxed and helped Sage when she felt uncertain, trapped in a corner, God encourages me in the way I should go. Both dogs experienced humility, in need of assistance, yet both were confident in who they were and what they could do. Likewise, when I humble myself before God and admit my need for him, he lifts me up, as he has promised to do: "Whoever humbles himself will be exalted" (Matthew 23:12).

Prayer:

Lord, forgive my pride. Help me to humble myself before you and surrender my life to you. When arrogance rears its nasty head and I'm tempted to motor my own speedway, thank you that I can look at the stars, the sunset, the mountains, the ocean, the plants and animals around me and be reminded that you created these things. You are powerful, you are mighty. You provide and care for me and you have given me eternal life through the humble life of Jesus. Thank you, Lord, for who you are and what you've done, and for who I am in you. I pray humbly to you, in Jesus' name. Amen.

12
Goodness

He has showed you, O man, what is good; and what does the LORD
require of you but to do justice, and to love kindness, and to walk
humbly with your God? –Micah 6:8

I sit on the edge of the small platform in the warm library
and wait for the children to arrive. They are coming to
hear my presentation about pets with disabilities. Sage sits
next to me with her rump on the library floor, as a dog given
the "sit" command should. Her ears perk up as excited child
voices enter the room. She stays in her "sit" position, allowing her nose and ears to pick up the scents and sounds. She
loves visiting schools and libraries, where she has the chance
to show herself off and receive an abundance of attention.
Children and families who have come to meet the young,
blind dog occupy chairs in front of us.

"Up," I say.

Sage stands up.

I introduce my blind dog to the children and parents
in the library. We then walk through the audience together,
Sage tethered to her leash, me holding the red nylon lead.
She allows strange hands to pet her.

"Hi, Sage!" Squealing voices call her name.

Sage is excited and a little nervous to meet these new

friends. Her back end wiggles continually and her tail beats the air.

"Stay close to me, Sage." I calm her with a few gentle pats.

Sage obliges and follows me through the room without trying to run off or stop to visit for too long.

"Good girl!" I bend down and pat her side.

I explain to the children that, even though Sage cannot see, she still possesses the ability to hear and that ability allows her to respond to my commands. I demonstrate how she "steps up" stairs by commanding her to do so as we climb three steps to a stage floor. Sage and I showcase the 'step down' command as well, taking the platform stairs back down to the library floor. The children smile and applaud and their parents join in.

"Good girl!" I reward Sage with a biscuit.

Those were words Sage heard many times. An eager-to-please dog, she relished my excited praises and gentle pats.

I, too, enjoy the feeling of having been "good"—doing work with excellence and treating people well. Peter encourages Christ followers to live a good life so that God may be glorified (see 1 Peter 2:12). Some people in my life make it difficult for me to glorify God in this way. I've worked with people who exhibit jealousy and don't want colleagues to succeed. Their undermining of others makes for a difficult work environment. Yet, showing courtesy and kindness to them glorifies God and produces a reward of well-being.

Evil—the opposite of good— is evident and has been at work for centuries. We remember early Christians fed to the lions at the Roman Coliseum and European Jews gassed in Hitler's concentration camps. America's own history is filled with atrocities, including the wars waged against Native Americans and the enslavement of Africans. Today evil persists in the world. Genocide and the sex-slave trade prevail. "Greed is good," echoes from the movie screen, taking root in people's hearts. Even the "good guys" are not always "good." Gone are the days of the old cowboy movies, when you could tell the "good guys" by their white hats. Those "good guys" and "good gals" are not as apparent, not in the movies and not in real life. Most hats are stained and dusty, including my own.

"Woe to those who call evil good and good evil," Isaiah states (Isaiah 5:20). When I see and hear evil, am I responsive or am I complacent? Sometimes I am both, my white hat marred.

Fighting evil is not like the movies with superheroes or larger-than-life cowboys and cops. Instead, overcoming evil with good as the apostle outlines (see Romans 12:21) can be challenging. But, it can be accomplished—not by human strength, but with the grace and power of God's Holy Spirit. Jesus did so when he spotlighted the Pharisee's hypocrisy and when he took care of the sick, hungry, and spiritually-malnourished. People flocked to be around him because of all the good deeds he performed, and because he genuinely cared about people. Do I mimic my Savior? And when I do good things, am I seeking the glory for myself or am I making sure that the glory goes to God, the One who is robed in white righteousness and goodness?

Even though I am expected to do good works because of the gracious, saving work Jesus did for me, it's not those things that bring me closer to God. Instead, it is God's goodness to me through his mercy, love and grace that allows me to draw closer to him. I then also respond in goodness to others. "As we have opportunity, let us do good," the Apostle Paul instructs in Galatians 5:10. He also encourages Christ followers to not grow weary in doing good. Though it can be easy to think that writing a letter to Congress condemning sex slavery in our country and around the world does no good, at least I've taken action. If I think standing against child and animal abuse by writing letters to the editor or publishing articles in print or online has no value, and therefore, I do nothing, I am not overcoming evil with good.

Though I do good works, I can never be "good enough" to earn God's grace and favor. "For it is by grace you have been saved, through faith—and this not from yourselves, it is a gift from God" (Ephesians 2:8). Only the blood of Jesus makes me "good enough" and only God's power can help me accomplish good works.

Similarly, Sage did not work for or "earn" my love, she was just herself. We shared time and experiences that drew us closer together. That bond was firmly set, like a concrete foundation, solid and secure. Her goodness came from within, and through that sweet spirit good deeds prevailed.

Sage received many "atta girls" from me, even when I asked something challenging of her. As a hunting dog breed, Sage needed activity, especially as a young dog. Since she couldn't hunt in the field, my husband and I decided to provide her toys that would simulate the practice and satisfy her instincts. We purchased a tunnel, usually used with children, and we placed biscuits inside. We left a trail of goodies, much like Hanzel and Gretel followed (in the children's nursery rhyme). Like those fairy-tale children, Sage followed the trail, using her nose to pick up the scent of the biscuits and following the crumbs through the tunnel. As a blind dog, she should have been apprehensive about entering the tunnel, not knowing the way out. But, she listened to our encouragements of "that's it, girl! Good dog, Sage!" and she enjoyed the harvest of goodies along the way. We purchased other scented toys to stimulate her mind and exercise her body.

Sage liked hearing "Good girl!" Likewise, I enjoy the praises from my Master, and therefore, I try to follow the

Apostle Paul's advice to "abound in every good work" (2 Corinthians 9:8), and I look forward to the day when Jesus says to me, "Well done, good and faithful servant!" (Matthew 25:21).

Sage's goodness came from simple things, and she exhibited that goodness not only to me, but also to strangers. She freely gave her attention and affection to people. She wagged her tail when meeting students in classrooms. She licked hands and faces in greeting. She didn't know these children. She was simply giving herself out of the goodness of who she was.

However, Sage was not always the most obedient dog. Her spaniel nose sometimes took her places I didn't want her to go. Occasionally in a classroom, she followed her nose to students' backpacks, sniffing them for the food they contained. During walks, she wanted to stop and smell the roses ... the trees ... the shrubs, grass, gates ... whatever had a scent from another animal. She wanted to investigate and she wanted to take her time. I didn't always have that extra twenty minutes to spend examining every blade of grass and leafy bush, so I would tug on the leash to get her moving. Did I let her loose and abandon her in the street because she was not being "good?" No! Instead, I gave her unmerited favor—and several pulls on the leash!

Similarly, God has to tug on my leash occasionally to get my attention and return me to the path he wants me to walk, fighting the "good fight of the faith" (see 1 Timothy 6:12). I'm not necessarily trying *not* to be good; it's just that sometimes other things capture my attention. Or, maybe I feel too weary to walk, and so I don't respond to the nudge God is giving me. More dirt on my white hat. However, just as I encouraged and helped Sage travel the tunnel, God dusts off my less-than-white hat and equips me for every good work (see 2 Timothy 3:17). It is because God is good that I can be and do good.

My glimmer of goodness only comes from the light of Christ. Like the beam from a lighthouse, God's goodness shines upon all creation; everything he created was good. The light he's put in me, his Holy Spirit, should shine upon all. In fact, Jesus instructs me to be a shining beacon: "let your light shine before men, that they may see your good deeds and praise your Father in heaven" (Matthew 5:16).

A little bit of God's light reflected in Sage. After learning that our adopted dog would become blind, Greg and I believed this pathway we began traveling would result in something positive that we could not yet see. We trusted in the Lord's goodness, that he would work all things for our good—and for Sage's good. We didn't know what that could be—but God did. He saw the road ahead, knew that I'd take Sage into schools and libraries and be able to encourage children through her life story. Those children, some with disabilities, those who were lonely, and others who were bullied, saw Sage. They heard her story, and they were inspired.

Sage and I could not have touched young lives in such a positive way without her becoming blind. A bad circumstance that worked together for good, a light that shown in darkness. Sage could not see light, but she was a light for the numerous children we met. Her goodness touched hearts, just as God's grace and goodness touches mine. The dingy hat became white again.

"Good girl!"

PRAYER:
Lord, may your image be reflected in my words and actions as I strive to do to others as I would have them do unto me. May I remember your goodness in my life when trials befall me and may your goodness shine in my life and through my life onto those around me. Amen.

13
Praise

Sing for joy to God our strength; shout aloud to the God of Jacob! Begin the music, strike the timbrel, play the melodious harp and lyre. —Psalm 81:1-2

The September Saturday sky gleams as the mid morning sun casts a warm blanket on the fading season. The browning grasses and drying willows beyond my backyard fence wave in the slight breeze. I pause from my autumn cleaning to soak in the view from the living room's large picture window. Sage lies on the concrete patio, absorbing the radiant heat. Front legs outstretched, her head is up, listening intently and smelling the season.

Greg is on a weekend outing with his best guy friend, so I am conducting a thorough sweep of the house. Spring and autumn house cleaning are classic American traditions much like Fourth of July camping trips and Thanksgiving visits to Grandma's house. After marrying Greg, I continued that customary chore passed down from my mother and her mother before her. But I take a moment to bask in the beauty before me. I discover a silent music whenever I partake of the Lord's creation, and this day, just beyond the chain link fencing, butterflies flutter around the yellowing

rabbit brush while black-headed grosbeaks and other songbirds flit and twitter near the meandering creek, preparing
for their annual southward migration. Nature's symphony
echoes in color and commotion a few yards from my home.

I return to my cleaning ritual, thankful for the slight
distraction. While mopping the kitchen floor, I hear *Ahoow!*
Ahoow! Propping the mop against the wall and going to
the living room window, I see Sage sitting under the cottonwood. Her muzzle arches to the sky, and another howl
emanates heavenward.

These are not howls of agitation but sounds of joy and
delight. Sage continues her September serenade, interwoven
with sprints and leaps across the yard. I soon discover what
causes her parading refrain: a squirrel scampers on the telephone wire above the yard.

The squirrel jumps to another tree. Sage indulges in
more howls and barks. I step outside to the gray patio as
Sage once again leaps into the autumn air. One of our
neighbors is drawn from the cocoon of her home. She stands
on her back step, looking at Sage. I walk to the fence, ready
to make a quick apology for my dog's commotion.

"I heard Sage's singing," my neighbor states.

I laugh. "I guess you can call it that."

"That is what I call it. Sage is happy and she's singing
her joy."

I can understand that. God's creation elicits a song from
my heart, and has since I was a child.

Growing up near cornfields in Burlington, Iowa on the
banks of the Mississippi River, I helped my dad set up wood
duck boxes and care for orphaned animals, including a stray
cat that stayed with us for more than ten years. I traipsed
the woods with my dog in search of owls and rabbits. I fed
the animals on our small farm and helped my mom with the
vegetable garden. I studied biology and ecology during my

high school years, and when I saw my first female park
ranger studying bison in Yellowstone, I told my mother,
"That's what I want to do when I grow up." I didn't become
a park ranger, but I did get to write about bison. As the
editor and reporter for the *West Yellowstone News* in Montana, I wrote innumerable stories about these and other
creatures of the region. I took a snow coach into the park's
twenty-below crystalline cavern to photograph the massive
beasts as well as the regal trumpeter swans swimming in
January's icy Madison River. I may not have been able to
withstand physics and calculus classes to become a wildlife
biologist in Yellowstone, but God directed my steps to live
next door to the famous park. The Lord enabled me to
combine my awe of nature with my joy of writing.

Ducks splashing and quacking at the creek direct my
thoughts back to the waning autumn's day. Sage has sensed
and heard my presence. She stops her "singing" and trots to
me from her station under the burgeoning cottonwood. She
sits next to me, as if enjoying the vibrancy of the autumn
colors, too. Though she cannot see, Sage seems to have a
certain "sense of presence" and a "living for the moment."
Her other senses provide the information she needs. Her
inquisitive nose and vigilant ears tell her things that her eyes
cannot, such as that I am now outdoors with her. I place my
hand atop her head and we stand next to the gate for several
minutes, enjoying the gloriousness together.

A mule deer doe saunters from the willows, munching
on grass still green from earlier rains. Sage's nose sticks
straight up, catching the animal's scent. She stands, stretching her long muzzle forward. I bend next to her and whisper,
"Deer." Just then the animal's large, twitching ears perk up
and the doe looks our way. Not frightened, she stands a
moment and continues feasting, walking a step toward my
neighbor's home with each bite. The simple beauty of a mule

deer doe still gives me pleasure and brings a smile to my face. I envision God also taking delight in the scene, and I feel an extra dose of warmth envelop me.

My mind drifts like the creek before me, recalling sweet memories of beautiful places I've witnessed, from the rolling hills of Iowa to the mountain peaks of the Canadian Rockies. The words to the old hymn, "This is My Father's World" whisper to me, and I feel compelled to listen to praise music—something other than my dog's "singing!"

I take Sage inside the house, find a CD, and pop it into the player. Hillsong Australia's "Shout to the Lord" resonates through the house. I pick up my mop once again to continue cleaning, listening to the words and humming along. Sage finds a blanket and stretches herself out to soak up sunrays streaming through the large picture window. As the song's final chorus begins, I stop my housecleaning chore. I stare out the window another moment, once again soaking in the splendor of nature. Then I raise my hands and worship the One who created all the beauty I see. Tears roll down my cheeks as the singer's words and the magnificence of not only what is in front of me now, but also of that which I've been able to experience in the past, overwhelms me. The power, glory and majesty of the Creator awes me once again as I watch the sun tenderly touch the grasses, shrubs, and trees in and around my yard, and I feel the Son, through his Holy Spirit, gently embrace me. King David's words resonate: "I will praise God's name in song and glorify him with thanksgiving" (Psalm 69:30).

King David was talented musically, creating psalms often set to music. Though I am not musically-inclined, melodies rise within me as I encounter the Lord's magnificent creation. I catch my breath as golden eagles soar above the Wyoming prairie. I shake my head in amazement at craggy mountain peaks with cascading, foaming streams near the Beartooth Mountains of Montana. My heart leaps for joy when thousands of sandhill cranes squawk and fly above the Rio Grande River in New Mexico. I sigh with delight while soaking up the sun's rays on a February afternoon in the Arizona desert. All this vastness—all of this grandeur—makes my heart sing, and often causes me to open my mouth in an *Ahoow!* (or at least a *Wow!*) at the marvelous splendors God has created.

From those years in Iowa to the many years I've lived in three different Rocky Mountain states, I feel closest to God when I experience his natural creation. I've visited Bos del Apache Wildlife Refuge in central New Mexico and witnessed thousands of sandhill cranes in flight. The resounding echo of a bull elk's bugle during an October evening in Rocky Mountain National Park is a sound I can never forget. Snowy peaks of Glacier and Waterton Parks glistened before my camera, and the sight of grizzly bears feeding or trumpeter swans swimming in Yellowstone still thrill me. The sights, sounds and smells of our national parks and forests thrill and touch my heart as the Creator himself whispers to and refreshes my soul. At those times I worship him for his power and creativity.

Sometimes, however, it's not a meadow of summer wildflowers or even a crisp autumn day that elicits worship from my heart. Praise sometimes springs up when I recall his kindnesses or his gift of eternal life. The music of the church—hymns and contemporary songs—also prompt me to worship my Creator.

King David knew similar stirrings. He writes many musings about praising the Lord. Scripture even records a time when David's worship of God caused him to dance in the street—much to the dismay of his wife!

*David, wearing a linen ephod, danced before the LORD
with all his might, while he and the entire house of Israel
brought up the ark of the LORD with shouts and the
sound of trumpets. As the ark of the LORD was entering
the City of David, Michal daughter of Saul watched
from a window. And when she saw King David leaping
and dancing before the LORD, she despised him in her
heart* (2 Samuel 6:14-16).

David certainly enjoyed praising God. His lifestyle was
one of worship. 1 Chronicles 13:8 records this version of
David and the Israelites preparing to bring the Ark of God
into Jerusalem: "David and all the Israelites were celebrating
with all their might before God, with songs and with harps,
lyres, tambourines, cymbals and trumpets." The great king
enjoyed celebrations, especially those dedicated to the LORD!

Sage, too, did her own dancing. She periodically pranced
and leaped into the air when she was outside and felt joyful
(and was chasing that pesky, scolding squirrel!). Her *Ahoow!
Ahoow!* reverberated through the neighborhood. Sage did
not jump inside (unless it was onto a bed or chair) and
she rarely barked indoors, unless she was looking for me or
expressing her happiness when I returned home. She saved
her "music and dancing" for outdoors, perhaps stirred as I by
the sheer adventure and splendor of nature.

Creation also spoke mightily to King David. He writes,
"Praise awaits you, O God ... who formed the mountains
by your power ... who stilled the roaring of the seas...you
care for the land and water it; you enrich it abundantly"
(Psalm 65:1-9). Perhaps when he looked around him, at the
mountains, plains, night sky, and creatures, or when he heard
the sea waves crashing or the stag bellowing, David was also
compelled to worship Creator God.

Although I am not melodiously talented, I do enjoy

the beautiful music made by others. My car's radio is most often tuned to the Christian music station. Hymns and contemporary praise songs touch my heart. I attend concerts and enjoy the band and soloists at church. But nothing stirs my soul to worship my Creator more than when I'm experiencing his miraculous creation. Just as Sage felt compelled to "sing" when she was outside—lifting her voice as a praise—so, too, do I feel prompted to praise the Creator when I experience the beauty of his creation. The majesty of God is reflected in the splendor of his creation. Paul writes in Romans 1:20, "For since the creation of the world God's invisible qualities—his eternal power and divine nature—have been clearly seen, being understood from what has been made, so that men are without excuse."

Walking a woodland trail causes me to listen. Sitting beside a blue expanse of lake helps me to slow down. Observing the vastness of a night sky makes me pause. All these marvels in their majesty and tranquility cause my soul to sing, *Ahoow! Ahoow!* And even prance and dance a little!

PRAYER:
Lord, thank you for the beauty of your creation that stirs my soul and for music that touches my heart. Thank you for the opportunity to worship you. May I ever praise you for your goodness and glorify you for your love and your creativity! Amen.

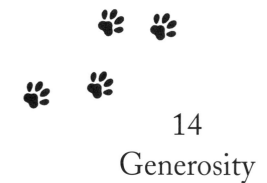

14
Generosity

A generous man will himself be blessed for he shares his food with the poor. –Proverbs 22:9

I'm getting close to the end of my presentation, sharing with a group of nearly one-hundred, fifth-grade students in a gymnasium. I scan the cascade of faces before me. How will I manage to give each of them the chance to greet their four-footed guest at the end of the program? Shaving nearly seven minutes off the presentation, by purposely leaving out some aspects of Sage's life, makes time for questions from the audience. These extra minutes will allow the students an opportunity to have a face-to-face meeting with this sightless dog who embodies the phrase, "Yes, I can!" and encourages them to push through their own disappointments and setbacks. Gripping Sage's leash, I head for the first row of bodies.

"I'll now take questions about Sage or about her story. I will lead Sage through each row, giving you all the opportunity to meet and pet her if you want. Remember, those with allergies to dogs should not pet Sage. So, now, who has a question?"

Sage and I weave between the rows of bodies, as the students ask their questions. I pause frequently so each child can reach out to my disabled dog. Sage follows, giving herself over to pats and pets, to hugs and whispers, hands and voices. Yet, she remains calm, following my footsteps and my voice as we snake our way through the gymnasium. We will repeat the scenario forty-five minutes later.

A few years after Sage completely lost her eyesight, we began visiting schools and libraries. I wanted to inspire young lives fraught with obstacles, whether physical disabilities or trials besetting their emotional stability. Everyone needs encouragement, and my blind dog was one way to dispense that prescription. "Be generous and willing to share," says Paul in 1 Timothy 6:18. By sharing Sage's story, I hoped to provide children a role model for facing their own life challenges. Indeed, many children as well as adults found Sage's story compelling. After one school visit, a third-grade teacher wrote to me and said what an inspiration Sage had been to a particular student in her class who was visually impaired. Hearing Sage's story encouraged this youngster to meet the challenges his own visual disability presented and, hopefully, spurred his classmates not to look upon him as less of a person for having such a handicap.

Generosity isn't just about donating money; it's about giving of oneself. Sage did that for several years as we traveled to various schools and libraries in our region. She willingly went along, exploring the classrooms and encountering the children. Never once did she flinch or hold back. The students piqued her curiosity and she investigated not only the room but also the people—and sometimes their backpacks and desks! One could say Sage unabashedly served the students by being herself and giving herself.

Jesus was generous, especially with his time. He didn't turn people away. Although he went off by himself at times to pray and to rest, he always returned to once again fill people spiritually and to heal them physically. He ultimately gave his life, the most generous gift he could give.

It's not difficult for me to be generous; in fact, it's one of my spiritual gifts. I enjoy giving gifts to people, and I yearn to financially help those affected by disasters and other life ills (Oh, to win the lottery or instantly become a millionaire so that I could be even more generous!). However, as both Jesus and my dog showed me, money is not the end-all to beat-all when it comes to being generous. Giving of one's time and talent and, most importantly, giving of oneself for others is also necessary. I have the same twenty-four hour day as everyone else; how do I use it to help others?

One way I give of myself and use my time to help others is by assisting animal rescue organizations. In years past I have helped my community's humane society with the organization's quarterly newsletter. I work with the staff and board of directors to plan and prepare the publication for distribution. I edit articles they provide, and write additional articles for them. I lay out the pages and ensure that the draft is ready for the printer. I also help various rescue groups when they need someone to transport a dog through my region, traveling between two to six hours to help a dog get either into foster care or to its permanent home.

Companion animals are not my only priority, however; God calls me to be generous with people as well. "The righteous give without sparing," says Solomon in Proverbs 21:26. My heart is stirred by the plight of abused women. I sit on a board of directors for an organization that helps rape victims. Poverty also affects me emotionally, so I sponsor children through World Vision. And I donate money when I can to children's cancer causes, and organizations that bring together disabled children and assistance dogs. I also give of my time and talent whenever possible because my Lord first gave them to me and he asks me to share his blessings with others.

My parents modeled generosity. Both gave of their time, talent and treasure not only to their church, but also to their neighbors and community. Mom often baked and provided potluck meals, and Dad helped with basic carpentry needs. My father also assisted with conservation initiatives, such as wood duck box building in Iowa and, after they moved to Montana, greeting visitors at the local wildlife refuge. Sharing meals with neighbors was part of my growing up years, as was sponsoring children in drought-stricken lands. My parents demonstrated to me what it meant to "excel in this grace of giving" (2 Corinthians 8:7). What a great example they've provided.

The generosity of others has benefited and blessed me. During times of financial crises, family and friends have given support with needed funds. During times of emotional crises, they have upheld me in prayer and comforted me with hugs and loving words. In times of personal struggle, listening ears and shoulders to lean on have been there. God has also blessed me with special pets, companions who have been there when I've cried so hard I thought my heart would burst, and when I needed someone with whom to share a great joy, such as traveling to the Bighorn Mountains for camping trips and hikes. Companionship is a generous gift, and I've been blessed to share wonderful experiences with different dogs who graced my life.

My first dog, a German short-haired pointer, lived on the Iowa farm with me for only a few years. He was born sickly and we knew he would never be a hunting dog, but he was a great companion to a twelve-year-old girl. We walked the woods around our small farm and hid under cedar trees to await rabbits and quail. We also spent many afternoons fishing at the pond. Whitey, named for his albino appearance, watched for the fish to jump, then splashed right in after them! We chased butterflies and fireflies together.

Whitey made me laugh. When I traipsed into the woods to write make-believe stories, this lanky dog accompanied me, and sometimes we napped together under the seclusion of an old hickory tree. After Whitey came Bridgette, the half-German-shepherd/half-fox-terrier mix, whose coat was like that of a coyote's. Then Sam, the stray cocker spaniel ruled my heart like a prince for nearly ten years.

Dogs exude generosity. Assistance dogs and war dogs don't hesitate to give their all for the one they accompany. Dogs everywhere generously give to their human friends, sometimes with the ultimate sacrifice of their very lives.

I will forever be grateful for the opportunities of visiting schools and libraries with Sage. Nearly one thousand children heard Sage's story and met this incredible dog, who shared her time and her talent with them. Amid the pats to her head and cheek-to-cheek hugs, Sage shared sniffs and kisses … encouraging those children to be who God made them to be, imperfect as we all are, but deeply loved by their Creator.

PRAYER:
Heavenly Father, thank you for your generous gift, your Son Jesus Christ. Thank you for the amazing blessings you bestow upon me, big and small. What a generous God you are! Help me to be a giver wherever you lead me to give of myself so that others may be helped. Amen.

"Cool!" - Playing in the wintry yard

"Where's that cat?" - Listening for the pitter-patter of kitten feet

"Oh, there you are!" - Enjoying Murphy's company

15
Wisdom

I will guide you in the way of wisdom and lead you along straight paths. When you walk, your steps will not be hampered; when you run, you will not stumble. –Proverbs 4:11-12

Moving cautiously through the living room of our new house for the first time, Sage sniffs the carpet and places her paws gingerly upon the floor covering. I lead her by leash, allowing her to gradually investigate her new surroundings. We travel slowly from room to room. I allow her fur to touch the walls and corners of each room and the hallway. After six years in one house, Sage now has to learn a new layout.

This house has two stairways: one down to the basement and the other outside to the backyard. Concerned how she will manage those stairs, especially to get outside to the yard, we practice and implement words familiar to her for navigating sidewalks, streets and curbs. We practice "step up … step up … step up," and "step down … step down … step down." By the fourth go, Sage has mastered climbing up and down the stairs, both indoors and outdoors. She seems to count them, rarely missing a beat. I am quite sure dogs don't calculate, at least not in numbers as we humans do; but she allows her nose to brush each step she encounters. She seems to devise her own clever plan to safely move up and down the steps. She takes each one slowly, cautiously, as if gauging the depth of open space in order to place her paw safely on the proper spot.

It's wise to be cautious. Proverbs 4:26 says, "Watch your step, and the road will stretch out smooth before you" (THE MESSAGE). This strategy kept Sage from tumbling and possibly from tragedy. Although she ventured through snow and grass on our walks, she preferred the well-worn paths of dirt roads and sidewalks. Her feet helped her understand where she was traveling.

Not rushing into things is always the wisest course to take. "Fools rush in where angels fear to tread," said the British poet Alexander Pope in 1709. The fools he spoke of were literary critics, but they can also be those who don't have enough knowledge to make good decisions, whether due to less experience or less education in the matter. Foolish, careless people rush in and attempt things that wiser, more experienced people will approach with more reflection and perhaps more success. Solomon would agree. He speaks often of the difference between the wise and the foolish. In Proverbs 14:8 he says, "The wisdom of the prudent is to give thought to their ways, but the folly of fools is deception." The wise person ponders before proceeding and asks God for guidance before making a decision or before speaking words that cannot be taken back.

Wisdom manifested itself in my dog even more as she grew older. Like people who have weathered the storms of life successfully, Sage matured in wisdom and learned from her mistakes. Humans can respond similarly, although I don't always learn quickly from my mistakes. Too much focus on the past can be unhealthy, but God can use my mistakes to prune and mold me, shaping me into the person he wants me to become, and get me back on the right track.

Just as I can turn my car around if I get lost when traveling a roadway, I can and should turn around when I realize I'm traveling the wrong road in life.

I learn more about life's choices when I read Solomon's wise writings. "The wise in heart accepts commands, but a chattering fool comes to ruin. The man of integrity walks securely, but he who takes crooked paths will be found out" (Proverbs 10:8-9). I've often taken meandering pathways in life, not always seeking God's will or asking for his direction. For example, I once moved to another state for a lesser-paying job, simply because I felt the need to leave, instead of searching for options closer to home and asking God to guide me in that decision. He helped me once I arrived and called out to him—he provided a second job to help stretch my low funds, and he led me to friends that I still cherish. However, I would have been wiser to have first sought his guidance instead of acting out of impulse. Perhaps he would have provided a better option financially and therefore, emotionally.

I don't always hearken to nudges to slow down—to think before I speak or act. I'm guilty of sometimes letting emotion get the best of me. Then I often regret my decision or the words I've spoken. At those times of regret I need to ask forgiveness from God and the person I've wounded as well as from myself. Dwelling on hurt and anger and not seeking a resolution creates even greater problems, and we are wise not to allow these feelings to fester in the first place.

Solomon, though he was the wisest king who ever lived, also made mistakes. We can read Solomon's laments in the book of Ecclesiastes and learn from his mistakes as well as from his wisdom. Life is filled with choices and decisions, and the Bible's truths help guide us along our journeys.

Examples of living wisely, both of my grandmothers lived to be nearly ninety years old. One suffered from

Alzheimer's and needed constant care in her late life. The other, however, remained in her own home until she died; though she received in-home services, such as housecleaning and meal preparation, her mind remained fairly sharp. I remember Grandma Mardy well. Her parents were Germans who had immigrated to the United States in the late 1800s. Grandma Mardy had a strong will and a determined demeanor, but she also knew the Scriptures and leaned faithfully on God. She lived through the Great Depression, running first a store and then a farm. Her experiences and her willingness to let the Lord guide her steps provided her with great wisdom, which she imparted to her only child, my mother. Neither my grandmother nor my mother let their emotions control them. Instead, they leaned upon the Lord and called upon his guidance in all decisions, large or small.

I'm still learning these valuable lessons. With each step along my own faith journey, I become more and more aware of my need for God. He patiently offers me his unending loving kindness. When I am unwise and make mistakes, he waits for me to turn around and allows his all-knowing wisdom and mercy to guide me in the direction he knows is best for me.

Solomon's father, David, knew the wisdom of following God's will and the pathway he lays out. Although David committed adultery with Bathsheba and had her husband killed, David later repented of his sins and once again was welcomed by the loving Lord. David knew firsthand about God's grace and forgiveness. I also can confess my sins and errors, heed God's guidance, and return to walking on his path.

It is wise to admit our mistakes and let the Lord do a course correction. It is wiser still to not rush into decisions or words. Like Sage, who learned to slow down and approach stairs with greater caution, I'm learning to practice such wisdom in dealing with life's challenges. At those times the still, small voice of God whispers, "This is the way, walk in it" (Isaiah 30:21).

PRAYER:

Lord, please help me to grow in wisdom. Help me to learn to listen to your still, small voice and to discern your will for my life. Guide me in all my ways and help me when I do stumble and fall. Help me to return to the path you want me to tread and to walk with you all my life. Amen.

16
Love

Love is patient, love is kind... It always protects, always trusts,
always hopes, always perseveres. —1 Corinthians 13: 4-7

Coziness envelops me as I lean back in my oversized recliner
with my green- and cream-colored afghan tucked around
me. Through the window I watch snowflakes like tiny white
butterflies dithering down, covering the earth. I slouch as
a whole-body shiver courses through me. My throat is raw
from coughing and my nose is red from blowing. I despise
being ill. The only uplift I feel is the fact that my black-and-
white dog lounges next to me. The warmth from her body
is soothing, and the tenderness of her heart reaches into
mine. Sage doesn't mind that I'm sick; she only cares that
I'm home with her. Just as I respond to her affection, she
also relishes my nearness as we snuggle. She wiggles as close
to me as she can, stretching lengthwise across the pea-green
chair. Having her next to me is like being wrapped in an
extra blanket, and I soon succumb to much-needed sleep.

A few days later, I am well again. Tea, soup, juice, and
companionship have helped me heal. Sage and I again sit
in the recliner near the woodstove. As a fire crackles and
blazes, I stroke her lean body, and I thank her for her warm

ministrations. I know that she loves me, and she knows that I love her. She lays her head on my chest, and tilts her head up. I look at those cloudy, blind eyes. She doesn't need to see to experience love. I run my hand atop her head and give a few scratches behind her ears. Sage sighs deeply and closes her eyes momentarily. Delighting in the company and the feelings we share, Sage and I sit together, bonded by deep affection and devotion. Like the woodstove's fire heats the house, the feelings Sage and I share warm our hearts.

The well-known Bible verse puts it succinctly: "For God so loved the world that he gave his one and only Son, that whoever believes in him shall not perish but have eternal life" (John 3:16). God's unfailing, sacrificial love reached out when his Son Jesus stretched out his arms on the cross and gave up his life. Jesus was the ultimate loving sacrifice.

Many people sacrifice their lives so that others may live. Soldiers in battle give up their lives for their comrades and for their nation. Firefighters and police officers place themselves in harm's way in the line of duty to protect their communities. Parents have sacrificed their own welfare for that of their children. Dogs think nothing of their own lives when they work to save others—in war, in rescue, in service, in love. Although Sage did not save my physical life, I do believe she rescued me, in a sense. She came into our lives during a season of turmoil for me. Great changes had taken place: a move, a job change, the loss of another dear dog, marriage, and having to live nearly 500 miles from my aging parents. As an only child, that's a difficult surrender. I was still becoming familiar with my newest community and feeling a bit lost and overwhelmed. Adopting Sage, then learning of her impending disability, helped me re-focus from myself to this creature that would become even more dependent upon me, her caregiver. I showered Sage with affection, and she flourished like flowers drink up dew. I, too, grow under God's healing rain of love, the showers of blessings he bestows, and the grace-filled guidance he provides.

God *is* love. God loves me so much that he blesses my life with many good things, including the gift of eternal life through his Son. God's love is not self-focused or directed to only a few. Scripture says he loved the entire world, therefore, if I claim to be his child, I am to love others as well. Just as Jesus stretched out his arms to die on the cross, I also need to extend my arms and my heart in a loving embrace to others. "If anyone says, 'I love God,' yet hates his brother, he is a liar. For anyone who does not love his brother, whom he has seen, cannot love God, whom he has not seen" (1 John 4:20). Loving God and loving others is not a suggestion, it's a commandment found throughout Scripture.

In sacrificial love, God gave his time, his healing power, his life to benefit others. Oftentimes, a parent's love is also sacrificial. I remember growing up in Iowa and wanting to be like other families and go to the local ice cream or burger shop. We were a one-income family, and my parents didn't have a lot of extra money for such outings. But on occasion, we'd gather on a hot summer's evening after church for ice cream with a few other families. My mother rarely ate the creamy, cool treat. Her sacrifice allowed Dad and I to enjoy something a bit more expensive than just an ice cream cone, such as a sundae or malt. And at a burger restaurant, what kid doesn't want fries? Mom would eat a simple hamburger so there was money for Dad and I to each have a burger and fries. It's almost hard to imagine these days, that a family of three couldn't really afford for all members to eat out at such simple places back in the 1960s and '70s, when burgers and fries cost less than a dollar each. However, that was our family's situation, and so Mom sacrificed in order for her husband and child to relish such a special treat. When I think of serving and sacrificing, I think of my mother, who continues to give—and give up—so that others may have.

Sage was also a giver. She stretched herself out alongside me that day I was ill, and she did so many times during the journey we shared with one another. She could not see me; she could not see the chair; she could not see the bed. But, wherever I was inside the home or outside in the yard, my blind dog wanted to be near me. No wonder *G-o-d* spelled backwards is *d-o-g*. God's love manifests through his creation—including the canine creature. Sage wanted to give her love and she wanted my love. God wants me to share love with others, the love he has for them and the love he's developing within me.

At times, though, I find it hard to follow Jesus' command to love other people. When someone cuts me off in traffic, I don't feel very gracious towards them. When someone doesn't follow through or doesn't pay attention to important details and creates an extra workload for me at home or on the job, I don't feel very loving. When people are rude or disrespectful, I may not utter a loving response but instead, fume inside and out. Jesus did not live his life that way. His steadfast love reached even to his enemies, and he asks the same of me (see Matthew 5:43-46).

Jesus, though he gave love, did not always receive love in return. In fact, the Son of God who deserves honor and esteem, endured mockery. He experienced betrayal. He died for the sake of others. Jesus suffered greatly—for each and every person who has ever lived. Yet, he bore these ordeals willingly. Jesus' life on earth reflected the life of a servant. His service displayed his love for people. He expects the same from those who say they follow him. My mother responded to that call. I would be astute to follow in her footsteps … and those of my Savior.

Loving others involves serving them. Whether I pray for someone, donate money to support an orphan, or give items to a safe house for women, as long as I do it from the heart, I am serving and I am loving them. When someone offends me, but I don't retaliate, I act lovingly. When I cook a special meal for my hard-working husband or treat my best friend to lunch, I am bestowing love. Yet, there are times when I don't act very lovingly and I disregard God's command to love. Servanthood is not an easy path, and it's a road that human nature doesn't want to trod. Yet, it's the road Christ took, all the way to the cross, and he asks me to follow him, even when it's not easy.

Love is an action, not a feeling. Christ was a man of action; he demonstrated his love for others in innumerable ways, especially in the sacrifice of his own life. Jesus tells me that, as his follower, I must do the same. He commands me to love others as he has loved me, and to take up my cross and follow him (see John 15:12 and Luke 9:23). I cultivate love because of God's love for me, but I have to share it and practice it—not just say the words or wait to feel the feeling. Love is an action and it's a choice.

That's how Jesus lived and it's how he died: he chose to act. And, he made that choice knowing I and the millions of others for whom he died were sinful, living in a fallen world. I cannot comprehend that kind of love, but I am grateful for it. I experienced just a small dose of such love living with Sage; and I was fortunate to have seen such love manifested in my parents. Yet, God's love far out-shines than that of my dog or my parents. His boundless, eternal, ever-present love has no beginning and no end. If God, whom I cannot see, can love me in spite of my shortcomings and sin, can I not share the blessing of his love with others, whom I can see? People blossom when love is showered upon them.

Just as Sage flourished in my love and care, through the power of the Holy Spirit, I, too, grow as a response to God's love and grace and then, by choice and action, share that blessing with others. So, how can I act more lovingly toward others and more fully understand God's love for me? By the power of God's Holy Spirit, bending my knee at the cross, and seeing Love manifested.

PRAYER:
Dear Lord, help me to act more lovingly toward others and toward you. Forgive me when I don't. I thank you for your endless love and sacrificing mercy. May your love for all your creation and the example of Jesus, who was servant of all, be manifested in and through me. Amen.

17
Loyalty

Keep this desire in the hearts of your people forever, and keep their hearts loyal to you. –1 Chronicles 29:18

My husband embraces me as I come in the front door, returning from an out-of-town conference that lasted several nights.

Then Sage calls from the bedroom. *Awhoo! Awhoo!* she bays happily. We hear her tail whacking the quilted bedcover then her paws thumping the floor as she jumps from the bed. Her flag tail steers her like a boat's rudder as she wiggles into the living room, body in full motion. Her happy howls echo throughout the house. Sage sets herself as close to me as she can get, clamoring for attention. Devotion prevails, and I'm reminded of the classic 1970s movie, *Grease*, in which Olivia Newton John sings "Hopelessly Devoted to You." Aren't homecomings wonderful?

After my absence of many days, Sage followed me everywhere! When I went to the kitchen, she followed; if I went downstairs to the laundry area, she came down, too. Even though she couldn't see me, she wanted to be near me. Her wagging tail and her excited voice welcomed me when

I returned in the evening from work. Even when I wasn't gone—if I was simply hanging out at home—Sage leaned into my hands for pats and pawed at me with her foot for some additional attention.

Daily news often reports the stories of dogs saving lives, offering protection from intruders, and traveling great distances to be reunited with their human families. What bonds a dog to a person? Dogs look to someone to be the alpha, "the top dog," and since people are the caregivers of their dogs, providing nutrition and companionship, the human is most often respected as the alpha. The more one positively interacts with a dog, the stronger the bond will be. Think of search and rescue dogs; yes, they are helping to locate a stranger, but they are also responding to the request of their handler. Loyalty is inherent in dogs; God created them that way.

Loyalty is demonstrated throughout the Bible. Jesus was loyal to his disciples, praying earnestly for them and providing for all their needs when they traveled. Ruth's devotion to Naomi, her mother-in-law, caused her to exclaim, "Don't urge me to leave you or to turn back from following you. Where you go, I will go, and where you stay I will stay. Your people will be my people, and your God my God" (Ruth 1:16). David displayed loyalty to Saul's family even when Saul tried to kill him. David was also devoted to God and he reminded Solomon, who succeeded him as king, to follow in his footsteps: "And you, my son Solomon, acknowledge the God of your father, and serve him with wholehearted devotion and with a willing mind, for the LORD searches every heart and understands every desire and every thought. If you seek him, he will be found by you" (1 Chronicles 28:9). Although David strayed from God many times, he still is remembered as a devout God-follower. So are Abraham and Moses. All are considered friends of God.

I can't say I'm always loyal to God in the way Paul describes: "Live in a right way in undivided devotion to the LORD" (1 Corinthians 7:35). Many things vie for my attention, taking my eyes and heart off of God. Those things can be good things, such as volunteering in my community or helping my husband with a project; but even in those situations, I am not to forget the Lord. Even if I just whisper a prayer of thanksgiving or ask for his help, at least I am acknowledging God and his presence with me. Sometimes my rushing around at work and home takes my attention off of God. David's words in Psalm 86:11 bring my focus back to Who is important: "Teach me your way, O LORD.... Give me an undivided heart, that I may fear your name." Living in that right way means living for God, being loyal in my worship and my walk and that means obeying his commands and doing his will. How I accomplish that includes spending time with him in prayer as well as reading his Word and asking for his direction. All of those things require commitment—an undivided heart.

Human beings are naturally selfish. We sometimes think our free time is our own, and want to pursue the things that *we* choose. The *It's-all-about-me* attitude pervades and perverts our culture; it's hard to escape the bombardment of *Me, me, me!* Yet the Christian life is one of putting God first, others second, and "me" last. Loyalty to the Lord and his way is not me-centered; it is a life of love and service. Serving others takes time, and God asks his people to give of their time for others.

Perhaps human self-centeredness is one reason God provided dogs, to teach us lessons in loyalty and selflessness. My dog didn't sniff out bombs or search for lost children. She wasn't an assistance dog nor did she do the job she was bred for—hunting. However, Sage gave me devoted companionship and deep loyalty.

Loyalty is a sign of a strong, caring friendship. David exemplifies such fervent dedication. As a young shepherd boy, he took down the mighty Goliath and earned a place in King Saul's presence. David played his harp for Saul and eventually became his son-in-law; David was also a friend to Saul's son Jonathan. When Saul became jealous of David and wanted to kill him, the two friends made a pact—an oath that their friendship would endure in spite of the anger Saul held against David. David's loyalty extended to others as well, including those who buried Saul after his death and to families who were loyal to the former king. It's difficult enough sometimes to be loyal to people who like me, but to be dedicated to people who are friends of my enemies? That's challenging, and that's Christlike.

Judas betrayed Jesus to those who would mock and crucify him. However, Jesus remained loyal and caring towards Judas when he said, "I no longer call you servants, because a servant does not know his master's business. Instead, I have called you friends, for everything that I learned from my Father I have made known to you" (John 15:15). Judas may have taken money to hand him over to the religious rulers of the day; but the rest of the disciples forsook Jesus in other ways. They left him upon his arrest, and Peter even denied knowing him. Their dedication to Jesus vaporized in the midst of fear; Jesus knew this would happen, but he still remained loyal to his followers, and he forgave them. Loyalty to one's friends means forgiving them when needed. God constantly forgives my missteps, and he never shirks his dedication towards me.

I have an office set up in my home. In that room I'm rarely alone; furry friends surround me. They lie on a rug at my feet or snooze comfortably a short distance from my desk. Often in the midst of concentration, I would pause and glance over at my snoring spaniel, who was completely content in my presence. She wanted to be wherever I was. Her loyalty and dedication rivaled most human friendships. It's no wonder dogs have been christened "man's best friend."

I continue learning to become more loyal to others and to God. Jesus and David provide great examples on living loyally toward others. So did my dog. God has given many steadfast role models whose devoted actions I can imitate.

PRAYER:
Heavenly Father, I am thankful for your loyalty towards me. You love me unconditionally and you bestow countless blessings upon me. Help me to have an undivided heart, giving you my all, and help me to exhibit the same dedication you have for me toward those people you've put along my path. Help me to be like David, a loyal friend. In Jesus' name I pray. Amen.

18
Faithfulness

LORD, you are my God; I will exalt you and praise your name,
for in perfect faithfulness you have done wonderful things, things
planned long ago. —Isaiah 25:1

The July afternoon sun beats down on our car with one-hundred-degree vengeance. Traveling the Wyoming highway after a visit with my parents in Montana, Greg turns the car's air conditioning on high. Still, our two dogs—Sage and our recently adopted cocker spaniel, Cody—pant heavily in the back seat. I point to a fast-approaching rain cloud. The midnight-blue oval reaches dark fingers to the horizon ahead of us. Greg pulls our car off the interstate, under the canopy of a concrete underpass. Unsure whether the cloud may contain more than rain, we wait for the shimmering screen to pass. With the shade of the overpass and the air conditioner blowing full blast, the dogs settle more comfortably in their seat.

Then the sky lets go and drops a wall of water upon us. It pounds the interstate like a jackhammer. Yet, from behind the rain cloud, sunlight still glimmers. Earlier in the day we encountered a rain shower that produced a radiant rainbow. As this fast-moving front envelops us, I watch, hoping for another colorful arch to grace our day.

Raindrops and hail beat a rhythm that rouses our two dogs in the backseat. They raise their heads. Cody stands to look out the windshield, and Sage, still stretched on the blanket, tilts her face as if sensing the vibrations of the pelting water. A torrential Wyoming rainstorm is an amazing sight. But along with it can come violent flash flooding of highways and small streams. Often, within the beauty of nature, destruction awaits.

The storm is gone in ten minutes, and in its place appears a vibrant double rainbow. Greg and I smile at each other. We pull onto the highway and drive through the desolate landscape typical of central Wyoming in July. But now drops of moisture sparkle on the sagebrush and rocks. Cooler air brings respite. The dazzling red, orange, yellow, green, blue, indigo and violet of the rainbow add a mysterious aspect to the high plains, stimulating our senses and our imaginations.

Rainbows remind me of the faithfulness of God. Myths tell of gold at the end of the rainbow, but the Bible tells of mercy and assurance. After the flood, as recounted in Genesis 9:13-15, God created the rainbow as a sign of his promise.

Promises seem to be easy for people to break these days. When we adopted Sage, and then Cody, we made a commitment to care for them as their guardians. My husband and I made a covenant to each other when we married. We pledged to be faithful to one another and to be partners in life. Our wedding rings serve as our rainbow of covenant.

How easily vows are broken in this world! Millions of dogs and cats are relinquished to animal shelters across the country, tossed by the wayside with less thought than a bag of rubbish; so, too, thousands of marriages and other important relationships that were once considered sacred, meet their demise.

I have known such demise. In college I fell in love and became engaged. Caught up in the idea of a fairy tale romance, I relished the tingling, fluttery sensations during dating, and dreamed of a future with this man. The relationship ended in heartbreak for me, the wedding canceled because of betrayal. For years after that, I felt lost. I had so allowed my life to be absorbed into his, that I didn't know who I was any more. Instead of learning an important lesson from the ending of that relationship, I kept following in my own footsteps. After a divorce and the demise of yet another significant relationship, by age thirty-seven I finally realized my faith in others and myself was built on shaky ground. Instead of relying upon myself and a man to whom I gave my heart, I needed to rely upon the truly faithful one—God.

In reliance upon others and myself, my heart's eyes were blinded by the myth that a woman is not a woman without a man. Then, while on a sequestered retreat, I came face to face with the real truth: a woman is not incomplete without a man—she is incomplete without God. The void I felt, the love I craved, could only be filled by the triune God.

Those failed relationships broke my heart. But God healed my brokenness. People fail one another, and they fail themselves. God does not fail; those who put their trust and hope in him "will renew their strength. They will soar on wings like eagles; they will run and not grow weary, they will walk and not be faint" (Isaiah 40:31).

Putting complete faith in yourself or "pulling yourself up by your bootstraps" is a mistake. My bootstraps were broken; but God, through his grace and mercy, mended them and continues to provide the strength to hoist them when they fall again. God renewed my faith, hope and strength during that retreat.

God didn't stop loving me. He waited for me, he courted me, and he called to me. When I totally surrendered and gave him my complete heart and soul during that retreat, he was there to welcome me, his prodigal daughter, back into his loving arms. God restored me, spiritually and emotionally.

At age thirty-nine, I married a man who has also committed his life to God ... and to his wife. As Greg and I approach our twelfth year of marriage, I more fully understand that no earthly relationship is perfect. Greg and I do not live a fairy-tale life even though our relationship is strong; it's our relationship with God that makes us—and our marriage—strong.

My spiritual eyes were blinded by physical and emotional love. Now they have been opened to many truths, especially to the fact that God is loving and faithful. He remained faithful in spite of my faithlessness, and he put me on the path he wanted me to tread once I committed myself to him. God sees the entire movie of my life; I cannot. Therefore, I must trust his sovereignty and believe in his faithfulness.

The great king David speaks often of God's faithfulness throughout the psalms, yet his journey was not always easy. He frequently feared for his life, even surviving in a cave to flee Saul's wrath and jealousy. He composed several psalms while living in exile and waiting to be crowned king. David's petitions to God reveal his belief in God's faithfulness, even during his darkest hours.

David's problems didn't end with Saul's death and his own coronation. His son, Absalom, betrayed him and overthrew his rule later in life. Once again, David was on the run, and once again he composed psalms in his exile. Despite his distress, David characterized God's faithfulness as unending. "Your love, O LORD, reaches to the heavens, your faithfulness to the skies," he writes in Psalm 36:5.

I may not be running for my life literally as David was, but run I do! My spirit runs when I'm emotionally and spiritually dry and empty, and my heart builds walls when it's broken. Amidst the storms of life, I try to captain my own ship, which, most times, leads me to the biggest rocks, causing the boat of my life to capsize. Then, like Peter starting to walk on water, then taking his eyes off of Jesus and finding himself sinking, I cry out, "Lord, save me!" God reaches out a loving, faithful hand to pull me from the murky waters. The sea squalls may still swelter and sway, but God can guide me through the tempest. The storm may not pass instantly; in fact, it may last for days, weeks, months, even years; but Scripture gives the assurance that the Lord is loving and faithful.

Greg and I pulled Sage and Cody from murky waters of uncertainty when we adopted them. Cody was used as a breeding male until he was nearly ten years old before being left at our local Humane Society. Older dogs have a more difficult time getting adopted, even if they are purebred like Cody. Though we provided Cody a caring home, his first week with us plunged him into anxiety and abandonment issues. He howled. He chased our cats. He left markings on the carpet. His biggest comfort appeared to come from Sage, for Cody was used to being with other dogs. However, Sage was not accepting of him.

Sage had been the only dog in our house for nearly seven years. She didn't take kindly to the elderly interloper. She growled at Cody when he came near her and she snapped at him when he tried to lie next to her. Since she could not see Cody, she could not read his body language. She was not sure she could trust him. She did not know he would be a faithful friend, so she "protected" herself with growls and snaps.

Perhaps Sage's trust of Greg and me waned during this time, too, much as a human child might think that Mom and Dad plan to replace him or her when a new baby comes along. First we had moved her to a different house; and now we brought this other dog home. What was a blind dog to think and to do?!

Cody proved himself faithful, however, and eventually won Sage's friendship. One day, he stepped between Sage and the large, looming elm tree in the backyard, where a squirrel chattered. Hearing that sound, Sage streaked from the brick patio toward the wooden fence that faces the alley. She was on a collision course with a sixty-year-old elm tree, much like the day she crashed into the cottonwood tree at our other home. Cody seemed to sense the disaster, and he scrambled his short legs to intercede. He veered in front of Sage, coming between her and the elm. Sage seemed to sense his presence, and she cut quickly to the left. Cody only received a glancing blow, but coming from a fifty-pound springer, it was still enough to knock the thirty-pound cocker off his feet. Instead of growling or snapping at him for being in her way, though, Sage seemed to understand that Cody had helped her. Thereafter, the blind springer grousing ceased—even on the bed. Sage allowed Cody to sleep near her and the two became great friends. Cody was in the right place at the right time to prevent Sage from crashing into the tree. Even when there are difficulties, "a true friend is faithful and loving at all times" (Proverbs 17:17). Cody lived out that Proverb, proving to be a devoted and kind friend.

Sage experienced many difficulties in her life, but my faithful guardianship of her let her know she could depend on me. And when I experienced setbacks, Sage was there to comfort me. She laid her furry head on my shoulder or placed a wet muzzle into my hand. My faithful husband also provides comfort and strength, as do my innumerable friends near and far. But above all, my God is ever present and ever faithful. I bring my troubles to him. I tell him my sorrows. I share with him my joys. I ask his guidance. I give him my requests. And he remains faithful always. Therefore, I have hope, whatever my situation.

God remains faithful even when people around me are not, and even when I fail. I may forget to feed my dog at exactly the same time every day. I may not take Cody for the long walk he wants. I may not finish a project or a report my boss needs by the end of the day. I may neglect to make an appointment my husband asked me to make. But God never fails.

Rainbows reflect God's faithfulness. And Sage provided an example to me of living by faith and not by sight. She was one of the most beautiful "rainbows" in my life!

PRAYER:
Lord, I thank you for your faithfulness. Even when I cannot see the road ahead, may my faith be in you, whom I cannot see. Help me to be more faithful in what I do and who I am. Amen.

"It's nice to have friends." - Sharing the porch with Cody

"I do like you!" - Snuggling with cat Murphy

"Nap time!" - Sage relaxing with friends Cody and Murphy

19
Respect

Show proper respect to everyone: Love the brotherhood of believers,
fear God, honor the king. –1 Peter 2:17

The kitchen wall clock registers 10:00 p.m. The night sky flickers with starlight and the sliver moon casts shadows upon the elm tree in my backyard. I gaze out the window at spring's nocturnal heavens and enjoy a moment of quiet before my pets prepare for what we call "nighty-night." Although animals cannot tell time with clocks and computers, mine seem to sense when bedtime comes around. At about 9:30 Sage and Murphy, our black-and-white cat, leave the living room and head for the bedroom. Murphy jumps on the bed and Sage lies on the floor. If I don't come into the room by ten o'clock, Sage seeks me out. Our routine is for me to take her outside to do her business, then for Cody, our cocker spaniel, to follow suit (I'm thankful cats use litter boxes!). The dogs placated, it's time to prepare their beds. For Cody it's a special doggie bed on the floor near the clothes closet. For Sage, however, it's the middle of the king-sized bed. Sometimes Murphy or her sister, Bailey, is already there. Nearly every evening, both cats are part of the gathering for the early part of "nighty-night." And if Bailey, the tortoiseshell, has already claimed the bed before her sister and Sage, I may need to referee a round or two—territorial fighting among sister cats exists, even after six years!

This night, Bailey has staked a claim on Greg's side of the
bed; sister Murphy rests at the foot of my side, and Cody lies
on his doggie blanket on the floor. There is room for Sage on
my side of the bed—as long as Bailey stays put, which she does
tonight. *Sigh!* No one is in foul territory, and no bickering ignites
among the players. I crawl into bed and manage to find some
space to lie down, surrounded by my little zoo. Life is good!

The two sister cats arrived on Halloween eve in 2005, their
mama having been abandoned at a friend's ranch. Our friends
coaxed the mama kitty from her hiding place beneath an old
grain shed and took her into their home where she birthed
six kittens. My friends, the Lunds, kept the mama and three
kittens for their ranch. They gave one kitten to another friend,
and two to Greg and me. When those kitties first came to live
with us, Sage could not see them, but she could smell and hear
them. Because of their size and energy, they seemed to "scurry"
like squirrels. So, Sage chased them. One kitten in particular
seemed to enjoy this. Bailey would taunt Sage during the chase
by hiding and springing from her spot, then bat Sage playfully
on the face and running while Sage chased her once again.
They played this game of tag for nearly a year.

Later, however, Bailey developed an attitude; she became a
bit of a bully. She and Sage no longer played chase, but Bailey
would swat at Sage if they were both on the bed at the same
time, as if she wanted the bed—and the people lying in it—to
herself. Bailey's sister Murphy even has to defend her right to be
on the bed at times. Cranky Bailey seems unable or unwilling to
share space with even her sister, with whom she used to cuddle
on the sofa as a kitten. If she swats Cody, he may growl. Murphy
(the sister-cat) will hiss or swat back. But Sage just turned her
head or even her entire body away and found another spot
on the bed—usually closer to me as if for protection. Bailey
doesn't respect four-legged housemates as Sage did. After she or

Murphy visits the vet, Bailey will spend several days hissing at everyone as if she's blaming one of us for the odor that emanates from said creature that has been to the doctor's office. Obviously, the blame should be placed on Greg and me, but the other animal occupants of our house are the targets of the scrunched up face and the aggravated hiss! Yes, Bailey not only carries a collar around her neck; she carries an attitude.

Sage did not possess Bailey's pouting, disrespectful attitude even though she endured many difficult changes in her life, from losing her sight to moving. She had to adapt to kittens in the household and accept another dog several years later. She took each change in stride, and she accepted and respected those with whom she shared her home, both two- and four-legged. Unlike Bailey the bully, Sage shared her treats, her home, even her bed with others in the house—even those who swatted her on the nose.

Treating people, including parents and government officials, with respect is instructed throughout Scriptures. Respect seems to be a dying commodity, yet God expects us to not only honor him as our Lord and Creator, but also to honor other people. "Give everyone what you owe him: If you owe taxes, pay taxes; if revenue, then revenue; if respect, then respect, if honor, then honor," Paul says in Romans 13:7. People are made in the image of God; therefore, when I show respect to others, I am also showing respect to God, the Creator of all people and all things. Likewise, when I disrespect people, I disrespect God.

Though I am to "place others above myself" (Philippians 2:3), that doesn't mean I don't value myself. I am a child of God, bought and paid for with the blood of Christ. I have been purchased with a great price. Therefore, I am valuable in the eyes of God. But that doesn't mean others are worth less. Since "Christ died for sins once for all, the righteous for the unrighteous, to bring you to God" (1 Peter 3:18), how can I be disrespectful toward people for whom he died?

Similarly, knowing that Christ died for me and that I am a child of the most-high God, how can I be disrespectful of myself? I am prone to negative self-talk, and that doesn't honor God, but it must please the devil. He is the great deceiver who whispers lies in my ear. If I cave in to those lies, to that negative self-talk, I am disrespecting the person God created, and therefore, dishonoring God. I am God's child through the death and resurrection of Jesus Christ. I need to be respectful of who I am in Christ. The old adage "God don't make no junk" holds true: God created all people; he has a great plan for each person, and all his children have a place in heaven with him. I am not junk and neither is anyone else. God values all people; so should I—and that includes valuing myself.

Respect wanes in society today. Polarity in American politics is visceral. Respect for those in authority has been replaced by rage and hatred. Political parties and practitioners spew vicious vile. Children bully one another at school and online. Parents yell names at referees if the call goes against their child. Colleagues defame one another. Even church members gossip about fellow parishioners.

Similarly, honoring parents and others in authority is becoming a characteristic of the past. When I was a young child respect for teachers and principals was paramount. Very few students crossed the line and back-sassed a teacher. Going to the principal's office caused students shame and trepidation. And if I talked back to my parents, out came the bar of soap from the kitchen and it went into my mouth. I learned at a young age to not talk disrespectfully to any adult. Now when I visit schools, I am appalled at how youngsters speak—to one another and to adults. Disrespect is dishonor; and dishonoring people dishonors God.

Dishonoring God is not new. God's chosen people, the Israelites often dishonored God by disregarding his discipline.

Throughout the Old Testament, the Lord tried to get his people to turn from their wicked ways, and on countless occasions he helped them as they endured terrible ordeals. Yet, time and again they turned away from him. By the days of the prophet Jeremiah, Israel was in dire straits: captives of the nation of Babylon. Jeremiah tried to understand why his countrymen kept turning their hearts from their God, who had delivered them from the bondage of Egypt. "O LORD, do not your eyes look for truth? You struck them, but they felt no pain; you crushed them, but they refused correction. They made their faces harder than stone and refused to repent" (Jeremiah 5:3). The prophet's heart couldn't fathom their spurning the one true God, and he wept for their souls and their plight.

Much of the same seems to go on today. So often I see people's stony faces as they express words of contempt toward others who are "different." That difference may be in financial status or in political persuasions. The difference may simply be in how one talks or looks. It may be as simple as how large one's church is or in how often communion is offered. Sage, too, was "different"; but that different-ness didn't mean worthlessness.

Am I a bully like Bailey, or steadfast like Sage? Everyone needs respect; God made each person and no one is better than another. I'd much rather be treated with respect and warmth than with disdain and rudeness. Why, then, is it sometimes difficult to treat others as I desire to be treated? Contempt and arrogance have no place in the Christian faith, yet sometimes Christians are the ones displaying the most disdain.

In contrast, Jesus hung out with the lowliest people of his day: grungy fishermen, unrestrained prostitutes, and the unpopular tax collectors. But he treated each man and woman with dignity. He met their needs, but mostly he met them as people—not with disdain, but with respect. God's children can and should do likewise.

PRAYER:

Dear Lord, forgive me when I disrespect others and myself, because when I do, I disrespect you. Help me to see the value in people as you value them, and as you value me. Help me to live with honesty and integrity, for then I also honor you, my Lord and Savior. Amen.

"I am a springer, you know!" - Trying to catch that silly squirrel

"This time I brought some help!" - Treeing squirrels with Cody

20
Self-Control

*Like a city whose walls are broken down is a man who
lacks self-control. –Proverbs 25:28*

Standing at the kitchen sink washing dishes, my daydream
is interrupted by two dogs barking in the backyard. As my
eyes adjust to the bright sunlight through the window, I check
to see what the commotion is all about. Sage and Cody race
around the elm tree near the back fence, yelping, and woofing.
Within a few moments, the entire neighborhood is filled with
the noise of barking dogs. The chorus includes the tri-colored
cocker spaniel next door, the beagle a few houses down, and
the basset hound on the other side of us—none of which can
see the old elm tree or its contents. Sage can't see the two
squirrels sitting in the branches above, but she knows those
long, bushy-tailed creatures are there because she smells them
and hears them taunting her with their chatter. That scent
and the sound of their scurrying feet set her voice in motion.
Cody can see those little tree hoppers, and he sets his face
heavenward in a spaniel howl, telling those creatures that he
knows they are invading his yard.

 After about six minutes of listening to my dogs and the
neighborhood dogs carry on (I give an extra minute for them

to tire of their own noise), I go out on the redwood deck
and yell at my dogs to be quiet. Cody looks at me briefly
then resumes his dodgeball antics with the squirrels and Sage.
Never sure if Sage will move out of the way in time, Cody cuts
from right to left around the tree, sometimes in large circles.
Sage senses Cody's movements, decides the squirrels must be
moving, too, and so she moves as well. How my two dogs
avoid colliding, I don't understand.

The basset and the beagle continue to do their thing, and
then I hear the beagle's owner literally scream, "Shut up!" The
beagle, like Cody, quiets a moment, but then starts up again.
It's just what beagles do. I hear another, louder "Shut up!"
I don't know which is worse: dogs barking and howling or
people yelling and screaming at their barking dogs! It seems
that no one has self-control, so instead of adding fuel to the
fire, I walk down the deck steps toward the tree. I stop my
two "hounds" from running around the tree and speak to
them softly. Then I lead them by their collars back up the
deck steps and into the house. Within moments, the rest of
the neighborhood dogs quiet down as well, and the squirrels
launch themselves from the tree onto a nearby telephone wire
and head off to raise ruckus in another neighborhood.

I give my two furry friends each a biscuit and coax them
to lie down on their blankets. Both are panting profusely, but
I sense a smile, like "Wasn't that fun?!" They are spaniels, after
all; chasing and cornering critters is in their blood. How can
I expect them to not do what comes naturally, any more than
the person with the beagle can expect that dog to not bay as
beagles do when they are after prey, such as squirrels? A dog's
self-control is limited, though it can be trained. Sometimes
people ask their dog to go against its nature, and therefore, are
not always successful in detouring the dog's instinct. Hunting
dogs are hunting dogs, and they will do what comes naturally
to them, such as baying and chasing.

God sometimes asks me to do what doesn't come naturally. He expects me to exercise self-control and to act with a new identity. The Apostle Paul instructs, "[Take] off your old self with its practices, …put on the new self, which is being renewed in knowledge in the image of its Creator" (Colossians 3:9-10). As I lean on and trust in God, I am being renewed and putting on a new nature, relying less upon myself and more upon my Lord. I then need to allow his Holy Spirit to work in me and to continually help me sustain control in various areas of my life.

Food is one of those areas. I've always struggled with weight issues, having been a plump teen and young adult. And chocolate is a major weakness of mine. My mother's chocolate cakes were simply the best! One of my aunts gave her a recipe that I still have in my recipe box. As a college student I discovered convenience foods and by the time my mid forties rolled around, snack cakes became my mainstay several mornings a week on my way to work. Schedules made it difficult to exercise, and since my body no longer had the metabolism of a twenty-something, the pounds piled on. Ultimately, I gave up, and now that I'm past fifty, my weight struggle is worse. So, I've once again embarked upon seeking God's help in an area where I need discipline. I know God will help me, but I also need to exercise some restraint and take responsibility. Through his grace, this blight in my life can be overcome.

Jesus knows my weaknesses. He, too, was weak and hungry after fasting in the desert for forty days. The devil tempted him with food and with wealth. He shot the devil down with the words, "It is written …" and quoted Scripture to refute the enemy's taunts (see Matthew 4). Jesus exercised self-control over hunger and greed, and he will help me do the same. "No temptation has seized you except what is common to man. And God is faithful; he will not let you be tempted beyond what you can bear. But when you are tempted, he will also provide a way out so that you can stand up under it" (1 Corinthians 10:13). Jesus understands my weaknesses and he provides a way to combat them.

Jesus' temptations didn't stop that day in the desert. The night he was betrayed, as he prayed in the Garden of Gethsemane, Jesus appealed in anguish to God, "Father if you are willing, take this cup from me!" But, he also said, "…not my will, but yours be done" (Luke 22:42). Jesus exercised self-control throughout his life on earth, even as he faced death on a cross, walking in the will and way of his Heavenly Father and serving as an example to me.

Food is not my only self-control issue. I become upset fairly easily, whether it's because of circumstances or people. Once ignited, my 'short fuse' is not easily extinguished. I definitely relate to what Paul says when he states, "For what I do is not the good I want to do; no, the evil I do not want to do—this I keep on doing" (Romans 7:19). This doesn't bode well for me as a witness for the Lord. Therefore, this is another area where I need his help.

Sage rarely experienced self-control issues. Her docile, kind demeanor proved favorable for her few behavioral problems. However, we did have to put the cats' litter box behind a sliding closet door because Sage's sensitive spaniel nose directed her to the source; she caused a few raised eyebrows when she was found digging up treasure in the box! But Sage never dug up flowerbeds or chewed shoes. We were never given a citation by animal control for our dog being a nuisance. If all I ever dealt with regarding Sage's self-control was barking at squirrels and having to clean up spilled-out cat litter, I'd say we had an excellent dog!

Cody, on the other hand, does have self-control issues. Like me, Cody enjoys food. He really, really enjoys food! Dog food, cat food, people food … he likes it all! Therefore, Greg and I have to be vigilant as to what falls on the floor and what Cody is allowed to eat ... and how much. He also experiences separation anxiety. When we first adopted him and would leave the house for work or to simply go to the store, he would sit by the door or window and howl. Taking him to the store with us didn't help much either; we'd come back to the car and find him, nose raised to the air, howling a blue streak! Fortunately, no one called animal control regarding abandonment or neglect! Cody has lived with us for more than four years, and though his anxiety has subsided, he still occasionally lets out a howl when Greg and I go out the door.

Cody's separation anxiety stems from a lack of trust. His former owners abandoned him after serving as their stud dog for more than eight years. He had to learn to have faith that Greg and I wouldn't leave him forever. I, too, experience angst when I don't fully rely upon the Lord, when I don't trust that he is looking out for my good.

I continue to grow in the process of living out my faith. God's power can help me overcome my various self-control issues, just as Cody's faith in Greg and I have helped him with his separation anxiety. "His divine power has given us everything we need for life and godliness through our knowledge of him who called us by his own glory and goodness" (2 Peter 1:3).

Peter and Paul both recognized that people have two natures: the divine, good nature which comes from God; and the human, evil nature that focuses on oneself. These are at odds with each other. They wage war within me. But if I continue growing in my faith by applying God's Word and seeking his direction in my life, I can call upon his power to become more self-controlled, and thereby to become more like Christ. God's power will win the final battle as long as I put my faith and trust in him and allow him to make me the new creature he wants me to become.

Self-control saves me from embarrassment and from self destruction. If I splurge on chocolate sandwich cookies with extra filling when I'm angry or discouraged, does it make me feel better or change my situation? The answer is obvious: No! In fact, I may become even more frustrated with myself for eating half the bag! And, of course, those cookies do nothing to improve my health. If I exercised self-control over the bag or the feeling of wanting to eat them, I wouldn't become frustrated with myself. And, if I'd at least exercise my physical body before or after the indulgence, I'd be better off! But I seem to be allergic to exercise—another bad habit I am trying to combat. Disciplining myself to increase exercise and lessen chocolate will most likely lengthen my earthly days.

Following Christ's example of not giving in to temptations, of keeping calm despite the circumstances or the aggravations, will help me to become more like him. Though Sage, Cody and the neighbor dogs put up a major fuss when the squirrels invaded the backyard, unlike them, I don't have to bark and yowl over my particular situation. Both dogs lounged more frequently on the back patio when they mellowed with age, and allowed the squirrels to come and go without giving a noisy chase. Perhaps they were learning a lesson faster than I am. Self-control doesn't necessarily increase with age, though. At any age I need the Lord's continual deep, cleansing work of grace.

PRAYER:
Heavenly Father, thank you for your grace when my lack of self-control raises its ugly head. Thank you for the example of Jesus who lived a life of self-control. I ask your Holy Spirit to lead and guide me through the various valleys of life—may I gain ground in the arena of self-control. In Jesus' name I pray. Amen.

21
Contentment

I have learned to be content whatever the circumstances.
- Philippians 4:11

On her dog bed in my home office, Sage snores loudly. I turn from the computer and gaze at her. Stretched out as much as her springer body will allow, Sage's head is half-on, half-off the blue and gray plaid fleece. Her snoring intensifies and I smile, cozy amid the contentment of my dog and the fire that blazes red-orange in the woodstove. Temperatures may be frigid outside on this February morning, but all is snug and warm in my home as Sage and my other pets sleep in their respective beds, enjoying the comforts I've provided. Though I am engaged in a flurry of writing endeavors, I pause a few moments.

After a splendid breakfast of ham and cheese omelet, I whisper a prayer of thanksgiving for the food in my well-stocked fridge and stomach. The teakettle is singing on the hearth and my videographer husband is earnestly working in his home office on a video project. Contentment wafts like the steam from the kettle and filters throughout my home.

I reflect upon my blessings. I also thank the Lord for safety the day before, as my husband returned from an in-state travel assignment, and for recovery from a flu bug the week before. Looking at Sage, a wave of conviction comes over me, reminding me of times I haven't been so thankful. A twinge of guilt echoes through my heart like a whisper bounces from the walls of the Grand Canyon. Here lies my dog that cannot see and has not been able to see for many years; and yet her snoring speaks of her satisfaction in spite of it all. I am guilty of feeling more dissatisfaction amidst the challenges of life than my dog that can no longer see or hear. I reach down and stroke her wavy hair. Sage startles momentarily and I pet her gently again and whisper, "Good girl." I know she can no longer hear me, but she doesn't need to; she recognizes the gentle, loving touch of my hand, and she relaxes once again, laying her head back on her doggie pillow with a deep, contented sigh.

Sage was greatly relaxed and comfortable in her familiar surroundings. However, after deafness afflicted her, when we travelled, even to places she had been before—like a friend's ranch—she'd pace. I'd walk her around the house on her leash, re-familiarizing her with the setting. Still, though, she wandered. I brought her blankets to provide a touch of the familiar; she refused to lie on them for many moments. An unknown army had infiltrated her comfort zone, and her discontent was obvious. An hour or more would pass before she accepted the plan of attack as outlined by her commander (me), a time for a short retreat from what was familiar to what was different. Sage would finally settle down and regain her contentment, for she knew that I was with her.

Contentment can be an elusive game plan for me, too, at times, especially when my comfort zone has been invaded. I don't always trust my commanding officer, God, when I believe he's given a greater plan to someone else. Like Sage,

I pace instead of relaxing and trusting in the Lord. Though I know he is always with me and that he will never fail me, I can be quite guilty of looking at my life's glass as half empty. I am not much like the Apostle Paul who said he had learned to be content no matter what his circumstances.

Sage, on the other hand, most of the time displayed satisfaction despite setbacks. When she first became blind, she rarely cowered from a situation, even when circumstances upset her routine and her blind-doggie apple cart. And though she may have experienced a slight setback at first, she adapted to new situations. She didn't howl in exasperation when her head smacked a wall; nor did she bare her teeth in anger because she was sick and tired of being blind. Deafness brought greater challenges; but still Sage marched forward. Her contentment despite her disabilities always made me look at her and shake my head in amazement. Sage was at ease with herself and life despite the lousy hand she had been dealt.

Many people know what it's like to be dealt a Dead Man's hand—the term applied to the set of cards dealt to Wild Bill Hickok prior to someone putting a bullet in his head. How often have I, like others, wished life had a rewind button, or at least a new deck of cards to play? However, Scripture cautions me to not look at life's glass as half empty, but instead to find contentment in God's many gifts, including his saving grace. "Godliness with contentment is great gain," Paul says in 1 Timothy 6:6.

The Apostle Paul experienced great joy and incredible sorrow. He planted new churches and suffered persecution. He coached new pastors like Timothy and died a martyr's death. This man knew both triumph and tragedy. Through all of his experiences, he learned the lesson of contentment: "I know what it is to be in need, and I know what it is to have plenty. I have learned the secret of being content in any and every situation, whether well fed or hungry, whether living in plenty or in want (Philippians 4:12).

This ability proves challenging at times for me. I see a friend's new car, and wonder why I can't have one. My colleague's husband sends her flowers every week to the office, and I ask myself why my husband isn't more thoughtful. Cabin catalogs beckon me to purchase moose quilts and cast-iron bear fire pits, and I want to … boy, how I want to! Boats, cars, spouses, houses, children, dogs … everyone else has a better one! But, do they really—or has God simply given me what I need instead of what I *think* I need? Did I need a blind dog? Obviously, yes, because I gained incredible insights through sharing Sage's life that I would certainly have missed if God had not led us to her. But plenty of people questioned Greg and me about keeping Sage when we learned she would become blind. God had greater plans than we could fathom at the time; our disheartened spirits quieted into contentment. We trusted our Commander and he's led us through joy and heartbreak, through the valley of fear and up the mountain of mercy. Living with a blind dog is a great challenge, but with God's help, we faced the difficulties and won the battles.

Yearning for something someone else has is called 'coveting' in the Bible, and it is listed as a sin in the Ten Commandments. Jesus and his companions grew up with and honored the Hebrew law. Jesus said all the commandments are summed up in this one rule: 'Love your neighbor as yourself.'" Love overcomes all types of sin, including envy (see Romans 13:10 and 1 Peter 4:8). *Whew! Are my eyes green with jealousy? And, what's that in my heart?* Reading these passages reminds me to repent.

Envy also happens to dogs. Some dogs squabble when they have bones; each wants what the other has, thinking the other one is better. Perhaps one blessing for a blind dog is that it cannot see what another dog has. Sage didn't bicker with Cody for what he had; she was content with her own bone or food. Cody, on the other hand, would watch Sage vigilantly. If Sage dropped her morsel, Cody dashed in to steal it. Likewise, he intently observed the tuna in the cat dish; he craved it. I guess I forgot to read to him the part of the Bible that says he shouldn't covet!

How often am I more like Cody than Sage? Desiring more creates idols in my life, and God's Word is clear regarding idols (Exodus 20:3-4). My lack of contentment displays a lack of faith. God's plan is different for each individual, and if I desire what someone else has or how someone else looks, I am in essence telling God that I know better than he does what's best for me. I make an idol of myself. Instead of focusing on what other people have or don't have, I need to be mindful of the gifts God has bestowed upon me, including the person he is molding me to be. Why is it so hard sometimes for me to see the myriad of God's blessings? Because I'm not viewing my glass from the proper perspective—how full it is!

When I gazed at my snoring, disabled dog, I was reminded that my life's glass is filled to overflowing! I am employed, I have a loving husband (although flowers are not his forte!). We have a roof over our heads (and it doesn't leak!), and we have devoted pets. I am also blessed with good friends and incredible parents. I live in a beautiful region of the country. Plus, I have a relationship with Christ that ensures my fate when that time of departure comes. I am blessed. Though I may have days of discouragement, times when troubles come that seem overwhelming, the words of the Apostle John encourage me: "Everyone born of God overcomes the world. This is the victory that has overcome the world, even our faith" (1 John 5:4). As I continue on this faith walk, my goal is to begin seeing more clearly that my glass is more than half full, for God continues to pour incredible blessings upon my life.

I wrote this from my friend's ranch. I observed mule deer in the field and heard wild turkeys gobble along the river. Sage was with me, lounging on her plaid blanket. As her snores deepened, my smile widened.

I am content for I have experienced the magnificence of God's creatures and the beauty of his creation from my own cabin in the woods to the incredible national parks and forests within driving distance of my home. My chalice overflows!

PRAYER:

Lord, help me to become more like the Apostle Paul, content in all circumstances. Forgive me when I compare what I have and don't have to what others have. Help me to see and acknowledge the many blessings you've given to me, and to be thankful. Through your loving power, help me to defeat the demon of discontent. In Jesus' name I pray. Amen.

22
Gentleness

*Let your gentleness be evident to all. The L*ORD* is near.*
–Philippians 4:5

With Sage's warm body nestled against mine, I rest comfortably in my recliner, reading a book I've intended to pick up for the past three months. Snow falls in large flakes outside my door this afternoon and a warm Sunday fire blazes in the woodstove inside the house. Sage has found a way to wedge herself into the over-stuffed chair. At first she lies quietly stretched out beside me. Then, as if she has an itch, she suddenly rises, turns herself around and lays her head on my chest. I pause from my reading to softly stroke her black and white fur. She sighs deeply and tries to snuggle closer. I pet her long muzzle and then scratch behind her ears, a favorite spot of hers. As I minister these gentle strokes, I tell her what a wonderful, loving dog she is. Sage closes her eyes, relishing the experience. I, too, bask in the tender moment. My hand rests lightly on her shoulder and we sit like this for hours—protected from the frigid cold outside—in comfortable, companionable silence inside our cozy house.

Throughout all the years that Sage lived in our household,

neither Greg nor I ever saw her act in any way but gentle. Even on the rare occasions she snapped or bared her teeth, that incident was caused by something that startled her, particularly one of the cats jumping on the bed too close to her, or, in the early days of Cody coming to live with us, when he invaded her space. Lack of sight meant that Sage needed greater personal space, between herself and other animals. She never snarled or nipped at a human of any age. Her gentle manners were welcomed in the classrooms we visited, and her sweet spirit continued to endear her to all.

Gentleness is a virtue not overly talked about in Scripture nor readily discussed in societal circles today. However, it is a character trait God desires in his followers, one that should be visible to other people. Peter says a person's beauty "should not come from outward adornment, such as braided hair and the wearing of gold jewelry and fine clothes. Instead, it should be that of your inner self, the unfading beauty of a gentle and quiet spirit, which is of great worth in God's sight" (1 Peter 3:3-4). He is primarily speaking to women, but gentleness is an attribute that should describe all of Christ's followers. Paul tells Timothy to instruct the male leaders of the church, "The Lord's servant must not quarrel; instead, he must be kind to everyone, able to teach, not be resentful. Those who oppose him he must gently instruct" (2 Timothy 2:24-25).

Gentleness brings to mind warmth and passivity, as in "gentle as a lamb." Lambs are meek and sweet. Most people don't want to be thought of as docile; they believe meekness means weakness. The culture says that a woman must be Wonder Woman and that a man should be the Marlboro Man, always strong and powerful and not caring about what other people think: Protect number one (self); be wary and cynical.

Jesus, however, did not live that way. Although he knew

where his pathway would lead him, he did not travel with a cynical spirit. He embraced people, including the lowly of his day. He was kind and caring, yet he also stood his ground when times called for a determined spirit. He often admonished the Pharisees and called them hypocrites. Not a mild word! Scripture also relates an incident in the temple when Jesus drove out the money changers. He overturned tables and scattered the flocks of animals being sold there. Jesus may have been meek, but he certainly wasn't weak! When strength and truth were called for, Jesus spoke … and acted. If I am to emulate my Savior, I, too, need to be gentle, but not so tenderhearted that I become a doormat. Jesus stood up for what was right, especially when it came to matters of God. Gentle Jesus stood up for his beliefs; I need to do likewise. Jesus was a man of strong convictions yet also considerate and tender towards people who were disheartened and disenfranchised. "I am gentle and humble in heart," the Lord says of himself in Matthew 11:29. There are times that call for harsh truth and times for keeping calm and quiet. I need to listen to the Holy Spirit's guidance as to when to speak and when to stay silent. The Apostle Paul also describes Christ as meek and gentle (see 2 Corinthians 10:1) and instructs his followers to treat other people with love and a gentle spirit (see 1 Corinthians 4:21). That teaching is sometimes difficult for me to heed.

I would not make a very good public school teacher. Although Sage and I visited many classrooms for nearly four years, sharing her story and coaching children about disability awareness and other topics, we were only with those children for a few hours a few times a year. Educators spend innumerable hours every academic year with youngsters. They need patience and a gentle spirit as they guide these young lives. God gives each person the appropriate measure of various character traits for he knows the calling he has for each person. My calling is as a classroom visitor who shares stories and important information—not a classroom teacher who instructs, counsels, and consoles. I tip my hat to thousands of people who enter the classroom daily, spending months at a time with twenty to forty young lives, and who do so with a gentle concern for their charges.

Jesus also truly cared about people, including children. He spent time with various people: He ate with them. He taught them and he healed them. He lifted little children onto his knee and blessed them. Wherever Jesus went, he helped people, and he gave them insight into the love of the Father. He spoke kind, encouraging words to people. He fed them, both spiritually and physically. The life of Jesus is a life of gentleness, and he calls his disciples to live their lives in the same manner. Paul tells his pupil Timothy to "pursue righteousness, godliness, faith, love, endurance and gentleness" (1 Timothy 6:11). To pursue means to follow. I am to follow Jesus' example even though the path may be difficult. Yet, with God's help and strength, I move forward in my faith walk and character development to be a better reflection of Christ; and that includes becoming gentler in spirit and demeanor.

Memories of my childhood conjure images of a gentle, kind and loving mother who took good care of me. I have similar memories of my mother's mother. They both willingly shared with others whatever they could and helped friends and neighbors. My grandmother cared for her diabetic brother who was confined to a wheelchair and shared her time with older people living in the local nursing home. Mom shared pies and cookies with neighbors. Both women possessed inner strength as well. They were loving and gentle towards their families, just as Peter describes women of God in his first epistle. But when times called for determination, both of these women exercised that quality.

Grandmother mowed her own grass until she was nearly eighty years old (though Mom and I helped her as much as we could!) and stayed in her own home until her death at age ninety-one. My mom willingly went without electricity or running water for fifteen years in order to live a dream she and my dad planned together. I realize I was quite fortunate—many people do not have positive childhood memories of either parents or grandparents, and I was blessed to have had both my mother and my maternal grandmother imitate the qualities of godly women, and one of those qualities is gentleness.

Gentleness is a characteristic I, as a child of God, should not only have toward my family, but also toward my colleagues at work and acquaintances I meet in my community. Yet, do I listen to God's guidance as Sage listened to my voice and allow my Lord to guide me toward greater gentleness as I interact with others? Do I share a tender word with those with whom I work? How about my attitude toward those with whom I disagree? Sadly, many times my thoughts, words and actions are not gentle. When someone tries my patience or is outright rude to me, I can be spiteful and defensive. But that is not the proper response. Solomon writes ever-applicable words of warning when he says, "A gentle answer turns away wrath, but a harsh word stirs up anger" (Proverbs 15:1).

Reacting negatively to an already negative situation only creates more havoc—yet that is often what transpires, even among God's people. Paul's instruction to the Ephesians is echoed in my heart when he says, "Be completely humble and gentle; be patient, bearing with one another in love" (Ephesians 4:2). Gentleness and humbleness coincide. If I am not tenderhearted and meek in thought, word, and deed, my pride is probably my problem. "Pride goes before destruction, a haughty spirit before a fall," the great king

Solomon warns (Proverbs 16:18). So, before I fall flat on my face in the mire of pride, my attitude needs to be one of gentleness—of the assertive variety, not the doormat version.

God is gentle toward me, and that tenderness should extend forth into the relationships I have and to other people around me. My dog's sweet spirit was not tarnished by disability and its accompanying dependence. Is my heart tarnished by life's battering ram, causing me to be more caustic and less tender? As I acknowledge my own disabling character flaws and attempt to walk more solidly in the footsteps of Jesus, God's Holy Spirit will work wonders upon those defects, polishing the tarnish from my heart.

PRAYER:
Dear Lord, help me to become a more gentle, caring person. Forgive and remove the pride within me. Help me to grow in the likeness of Jesus, being gentle in spirit and steadfast in your truth. Amen.

23
Kindness

'With everlasting kindness I will have compassion on you', says the
LORD your Redeemer. —Isaiah: 54:8

The third-grade students sit on the wooden floor in five
rows of six. Many fidget from the floor's hardness and from
being in my blind dog's presence. Sage stands beside me,
her sightless eyes scanning the classroom as though she can
see, her head cocked to one side listening intently. Suddenly,
she stands and wanders to a boy who sits motionless nearby,
his face tight and emotionless. Sage sits beside him quietly,
and then she nudges his shoulder with her muzzle. The boy
slowly brings his hand up to her head and begins to pet
Sage. She leans her body into his and rests her head in his
hand. Then she raises a front paw and stretches it forward,
as in a handshake. The young boy clasps her paw in his
hand then puts his arm around her body. They sit in quiet
companionship for several minutes. When I ask for questions from the audience, the boy raises his hand and says
softly, "I like your dog."

In the years before her deafness, Sage often traveled
with me when I conducted speaking engagements. We

visited classrooms and libraries, and I spoke about disabilities in pets and people and overcoming challenges that life presents. Sage was my living example. During those visits, Sage seemed to sense when someone in the room was in need, and she had the capacity to break through their unspoken wall of sadness. When that sense came to her, she would quietly walk to a particular child and sit next to him or her. Her presence and acceptance often compelled the child to reach out and touch her. Sometimes it was a simple pat to her side or head. Sometimes an arm encircled her shoulders in a hug. On one occasion a girl gave Sage a full body hug. Whatever the student's need, Sage met it with affectionate kindness.

After her retirement from school and library visits, Sage's kindness simply extended to her human family at home or to those who would visit our house. Cody also seems to have this particular capability. I recall one visit my parents made at Christmastime. My mother had been struggling with her health that year, and though she said little about being in pain, Cody walked over to her one day as she sat in one of the living room recliners. He reached his front legs up and leaned his body into my mother's, giving her what we call a "Cody hug." In response, Mom put her arms around the thirty-two-pound mass covered with fur and pressed her cheek to his. Mom was genuinely touched by Cody's affection and perception, and she whispered a word of thanks to him. A few moments later, Cody returned to his doggie blanket on the living room floor and went to sleep. Mom and I still smile at the memory of this little dog's sensitivity and his kind response to her arthritic ache.

I don't generally find it difficult to be kind to other people. I respond with an internal groan when I hear the plight of natural disaster victims in my community and around the world. I do my best to be as generous as I can.

I don't think twice about purchasing gifts for people I love. Yet, when it comes to the daily grind, I can be curt toward others. I sometimes allow the day-to-day events in my life to impact how I treat other people. The waitress at a restaurant may receive a minimal tip if I perceive her to be slow. Or I may grump at the grocery store clerk if I've become impatient with the person in front of me. In both cases, they, too, may be having a trying day; but instead of being understanding, I become critical. I don't listen to Jesus whispering to me, "In everything, do to others what you would have them do to you" (Matthew 7:12). This is the Golden Rule. But how often do I practice it?

I read in my local paper about the effects of bullying. That type of behavior doesn't stop at the school building. Now there is also cyber-bullying on blogs, cell phones, and social networking sites. That kind of harassment takes its toll, affecting a young person's school and work performance. Emotionally devastating, this type of anti-Golden Rule can even result in suicide. Though kindness should reign, cruelty often governs our culture, from the school building to the political office. Mean-spirited finger waggers spar for my vote, but instead, turn me off. So I have to question myself: how many people am I turning off with my own thinly-veiled disdain?

Can I not give a smile to the person in front of me at the grocery store? Should I not offer an encouraging word to my colleague at work? Can't I say a simple, courteous "please" and "thank you" to the one serving me in a restaurant, even if that's at my local fast-food place? Simple politeness expresses kindness, and the price of such benevolence is nothing. I can certainly afford to share a smile or an encouraging remark. Most people feel a burden lifted when someone gives them a sincere, warm smile or word. Scripture reminds me that I can brighten someone's day and lift someone's spirit by simply providing a kind gesture or statement. "An anxious heart weighs a man down, but a kind word cheers him up" (Proverbs 12:25). Whenever I feel down or defeated and someone offers encouragement in a word or hug, I experience relief, as if a weight has been removed. Simply put, I feel cared about.

Human and animal shelters are filled with those who have suffered abuse. Although I could never see myself physically harming someone, my cutting words inflict emotional pain as much as a punch causes physical pain. It's financially impossible for me to donate money to every worthy cause around the world or even within my own community. However, money is not the issue in the cause of kindness. The issue is about what is in my heart.

Sage showed kindness and caring, especially with children. She couldn't see their faces or read their body language; she just accepted the presence of people with sincerity and tolerance, despite strange voices and smells. She didn't judge people as humans do, based on race, religion, gender or financial status. Sage freely gave of herself to others. She practiced the Golden Rule. She couldn't see to whom she was giving, but the "whom" didn't matter to her. Sage's kindly affection was offered to all, and most received it with open arms and huge smiles.

The spiritual gift of encouragement is a present that I need to not selfishly withhold. The gift is quite meaningful to a person who is discouraged emotionally or disheartened by disease. Cody and Sage served as therapy pets even though neither had been formally trained. Sage showered affection on strangers and upon loved ones. Cody's people of choice are the humans he knows and cares about—especially my husband, my mother or me. If I am physically or emotionally ill, Cody spends time near me, either sleeping at my feet or somewhere nearby. After my parents' hospitalization in 2009, Sage and I stayed with them for several weeks, and her sense of being needed kicked into high gear. She faithfully sat beside my dad during the evenings and just let him pet and talk to her. She sat quietly, without judgment or expectation. She was just Sage, a devoted, kind-spirited dog that seemed to know my dad needed to have her nearby as much as she relished the attention. Like Cody, Sage didn't have the formal title of "therapy dog," but she seemed to know when she should assume that role, and she did it without hesitation or command.

Everyone needs kindness and encouragement. The human spirit is not meant to live in isolation from the caring spirit of other people nor to live cut off from the kind spirit of God. But many people try. Yet, Paul says it's God's kindness that leads people to him (see Romans 2:4).

As a Christ follower, I am to care about others. If I claim to live for God and love him, I cannot live selfishly. His love for me and kindness towards me overflow so that I can treat others with compassion and empathy—the way I want others to treat me. Kindness is displayed in many forms. Perhaps it's a phone call to a friend I've not spoken with for several months or even years. Maybe it's a donation to the local rescue mission or animal shelter. Or it could be serving my elderly neighbor by shoveling snow or mowing her lawn. Kindness comes through many acts, but whatever form it takes, kindness always reflects the face of God to others.

The gift of salvation is God's greatest gift, offered freely—much like Sage selflessly giving her comfort to those she sensed were in need. God knows I am in need, and he graciously extends his heart of kindness to me by stretching his arms on a rugged cross and enfolding me in a nail-scarred embrace. May I impart kindness upon others as the Lord, and my dogs, have bestowed upon me.

PRAYER:

Heavenly Father, thank you for the incredible kindness you've showered upon me. Thank you for the numerous blessings you've given, especially for the gift of your son, Jesus. Help me to treat others more kindly, even sharing such simple things as a smile or an encouraging word. As you have reached out to me, help me to reach out to others. Amen.

24
Hope

Be strong and take heart, all you who hope in the LORD.
—Psalm 31:24

I stand hungrily at the stove, relishing the aroma of chicken simmering in olive oil with rosemary and basil as I prepare our evening dinner. As I stir the browning chunks of meat, I glance to the left; I am not alone. In the doorway sits a cute, black-and-white springer spaniel. Sage maneuvered her way from the living room, where, less than two minutes ago, I left her sleeping soundly on her red-and-black plaid bed. She is drawn to the sizzling food just as hummingbirds are attracted to the honeysuckle blossoms in my front yard. Her Spaniel nose, created to follow scents in a grassy field, picks up the slightest smell of food, whether that be people food or dry kibble and biscuits made for dogs. Today, the fragrance of frying chicken wafts through the corridors of our home and lures Sage from her sleepy hollow in a room seventy-five feet away. She shuffles ever so close to me and the aromatic temptations before lifting that long, black muzzle for an even deeper sniff. Her hope is high that something will come from my hand or fall to the floor so she can gobble it up. She won't receive a food reward directly from the stove as she would like, though. The chunks of meat would be too hot to handle and burn her tongue! I let Sage sniff the air and nuzzle still closer, as if that would change my mind. But I won't be surprised if she happens to get a meaty morsel after Greg and I sit down to eat!

Sage never used to beg; she always patiently waited for a table-scrap treat until after the people were finished eating. However, in her older age her nose warped into overdrive—she could smell the most miniscule scent, and when my husband and I would sit down at the table, her paw would hit our legs constantly. Until she got a taste of what her ultra-sensitive nostrils were smelling, she wouldn't be satisfied. Cody sits by our dining table in anticipation, but he doesn't get as demanding as Sage did—most times!

My dogs' hope for food could be compared to my anticipation of a heavenly home, as well as the optimism I have in my current life on earth. My hope is in God alone, not in myself or in things of this world, which will pass away. Christ living in me, the work of his Holy Spirit, spurs me to hope for a better future someday. Maybe in this life, but most certainly in the life to come!

When tough situations arise, hope can diminish. Yet, in the Psalms, I find encouragement to hold on to hope in spite of my circumstances and feelings. "Why are you downcast, O my soul? Why so disturbed within me? Put your hope in God, for I will yet praise him, my Savior and my God" (Psalm 42:5, 11). David, who wrote many of the Psalms, had plenty of reasons to be downcast and to give up hope. People were out to kill him, and sometimes he made some really bad decisions. David may have come to a place of discouragement and defeat, but he never stayed there—he sought the Lord's help and forgiveness, and he found reason to hope again. "Find rest, O my soul, in God alone; my hope comes from him," pens David in Psalm 62:2.

David said that he would praise God for as long as he lived. Perhaps David didn't feel like praising God while in the desert, but he did so anyway. I know what living alone in the desert is all about—not literally, but certainly emotionally and spiritually. During a dry season in my life, I lost a good-paying full-time job around the same time that my husband's business came to a standstill—and this happened right after purchasing a new home. We scrambled and scrimped, but life was difficult. After several months of part-time work and new innovations my husband put into place for his business, we walked out of the financial heat, but not before receiving some distressing letters from the mortgage company. Although we were fortunate not to lose our home, the sand dunes of this season were hard to get beyond. Praise did not well up in my heart back then. Like many others, I sometimes find it difficult to praise the Lord while wandering the desert. The Apostle Peter, who experienced his own difficulties, encourages me to praise God, in whatever season of life I'm facing, because of who I am in Christ: "But you are a chosen people, a royal priest-hood, a holy nation, a people belonging to God, that you may declare the praises of him who called you out of dark-ness into his wonderful light" (1 Peter 2:9). Hopeful people praise God, and a praising person lives in hope!

I have hope because God gave me Jesus, who shed his blood for me. Though I may not be able to see or touch him, I know he lives and that I can also live forever with him. "Now faith is being sure of what we hope for and certain of what we do not see" (Hebrews 11:1). Hebrews is filled with "hope statements," encouraging me to not waver in my faith, and reminding me of all those people who went before me and stood steadfast in their faith. The writer of the book of Hebrews recalls the lives of Old Testament prophets and leaders like Moses, David, and Isaiah who stood on their faith. Likewise, Christian martyrs such as the apostles Peter, Paul, and James held fast to their belief that, in the end, they would live with God and the Messiah Christ for all eternity. That is also my hope—that despite my circumstances on this earth, God loves me and he's given an eternal promise, if I just put my faith and hope in him and not in the things and people of this world.

Hope is a stimulator, giving me something to look forward to in the future, much like the hope of chicken dinner stimulates dogs! No one can really exist without some kind of hope. There are times in this life when our existence is difficult. But, as many writers of the Bible state, praise be to God! For our hope is in him. "Praise be to the God and Father of our Lord Jesus Christ! In his great mercy he has given us new birth into a living hope through the resurrection of Jesus Christ from the dead, and into an inheritance that can never perish, spoil or fade—kept in heaven for you" (1 Peter 1:3-4).

Sage didn't just wait with hope for food; she also waited with hope for a walk. During all the years we spent together, she knew we took a walk nearly every morning. She waited anxiously near the front door, anticipating a leisurely walk, especially on warm spring days. Likewise, I wait expectantly and hopefully for the promise of life ever after with my Lord—for eternal springtime! He desires everyone to have that hope. I'm thankful to have this blessed future to anticipate.

My dog traveled an uncertain path in her darkened world, yet waited in hopeful expectation for special gifts from me. I, too, often travel an uncertain road in this darkened earthly life; yet I possess hope in the special gift God has given: His Son, Jesus Christ!

PRAYER:

Dear Lord, thank you for the hope I have in Christ, the hope that extends beyond my circumstances, the hope that means eternal life with you. Help me to hold onto that hope when waves of discouragement crash upon me, when darkness surrounds me, and all hope seems lost. Thank you that you are with me always, that you are my rock and shield. My hope rests in you, O Lord! Amen.

25
Peace

I have told you these things, so that in me you may have peace.
In this world you will have trouble. But take heart! I have
overcome the world. –John 16:33

Through the old-style pane windows filtered sun bathes my
home office and caresses the parquet floor. Sage lies quietly
at my feet, sun rays saturating her long black-and-white fur.
Her body casts a shadow on the floor as she turns slightly
to escape the increasing warmth. I hear her sigh deeply and
watch as she wiggles her body closer to me, enfolding my
feet with her length. I reach down to pat her stomach and
she raises her head at my touch.

Contact, whether from my stroking her fur or from a
ray of sunlight on her body, is important to my blind dog,
especially now in her older age and with the added disability
of deafness. Sage feels the sunshine on her shoulders but
doesn't see the light streaming through the windows. She
feels the loving touch from people, and senses their moods,
but cannot see their faces or hear their voices. I sometimes
wonder if she misses being able to see. I do know that
losing her hearing was difficult for her at first. However,
if she regrets either loss now, she gives no indication. Her

positive attitude is reflected through her wagging tail and affectionate cuddles. Sage possesses a peace in her situation that I'm not sure I would have if I lost my sight, my hearing or both.

The day passes in quiet companionship. Sage stays close to me throughout the day, lying in one of her favorite spots: on a rug near my feet. Occasionally, she inches herself closer, and at one point she lays her head on my stockinged feet. I reach down to pat her head and scratch her chin. Sage sighs. I smile. Peace prevails in my home and in my heart.

That is not always the case. Like most people who work outside the home, stress can be my constant companion, as I attempt to balance my life between work and home, and interact with people in both places. Working at jobs that involve the public or just simply having co-workers in an office setting can be taxing on the mind, spirit and body. People can steal one another's peace. Peace often eludes me as I juggle the many plates of life, with people and situations, and even as I deal with my own self.

Peace can be a difficult treasure to find. But scripture tells us to look beyond our difficulties, to dig a bit deeper, and we will find the richness of God's peace to help us endure. Then "the peace of God, which transcends all understanding, will guard your hearts and your minds in Christ Jesus," Paul says in Philippians 4:7.

Horatio Spafford faced one of the most awful situations a person could endure: the death of all of his daughters in a shipwreck in 1873. How could he find peace in the midst of those circumstances? Yet, it was then that Spafford penned these lines:

When peace like a river attendeth my way,
when sorrows like sea billows roll;

whatever my lot, thou hast taught me to say:
It is well, it is well with my soul.

Those words continue to be sung as a hymn in churches
throughout the world. I've sung those words. But when sea
waves crash upon the shore of my life, it is not as easy for me
to live out the words as it is to sing them. Instead of relying
upon the peace of God that transcends all understanding, I
attempt to find peace within my own self, to work at the
problem instead of letting God work within the problem.
Most times I discover that the real problem is me. If I would
more often "let go and let God" as the saying goes, I would
not only find greater peace, but also greater strength.

The peace that Sage exhibited did not come readily.
Sometimes she was in disarray, like an overturned applecart.
Three months after coming to live with us, we took her on
an overnight trip, staying at a motel. It was her first time
traveling with us. Just when she was finally familiar with her
new home and her new family, we took her away from her
comfort zone. My husband, a videographer, was working on
a project this particular weekend, and Sage and I went with
him. After spending a few hours videotaping, we found a
motel, grabbed a few burgers for dinner and headed to the
room. Sage traveled well in the car, but once we entered
the motel room, she paced. She only nibbled at her dinner.
We tried to settle her down with a chew stick and a few
biscuits, but even those treats did not capture her attention.
She whined and paced, paced and whined. We took her
outdoors for a walk around the motel, which was set apart
from the community proper and had a bit of open space
nearby. Sage seemed to enjoy the little stroll and after we
returned to the room, she ate her dinner and munched on
the crunchy stick.

We thought all was right again, so Greg and I prepared

for bed. We learned quickly what parents of newborns learn … your youngsters don't always sleep when you want them to! None of us slept much that night as Sage either could not or would not settle down. She would lie down, get up, pace, and lie down again. Then she would get up, pace and whine, and lie back down. She was like that all night. Greg and I took her outside at least twice each before sunup, thinking that perhaps she needed to go out. Driving home the next day, Sage slept as soundly as you please in the car as Greg and I tried to keep our eyes open and stay safe on the road.

Peace comes from trust and trust comes with time. In the travels and road trips thereafter, Sage never again was as restless as she was that night. Between losing her eyesight, leaving the home she'd just recently adjusted to, and having to stay at a place that was completely unfamiliar to her, Sage had every reason to be upset. Even though we were with her, the strange room with its strange smells and sounds made her restless and not at peace with the situation. She had not yet learned to trust us in all circumstances. Sometimes in my faith walk I am restless like Sage was in the motel room. I do not implement complete faith and trust in my caregiver, God, and therefore, when uncomfortable, unfamiliar situations arise, peace alludes me as it did Sage that night.

Other circumstances would periodically steal Sage's peace, including when Cody first came to live with us. Sage's reaction was defensive. Sometimes my reaction to adverse circumstances is also one of defense. When the tsunami of circumstances crashes in—through the unexpected death of loved ones, financial upheaval, undiagnosed health problems, or other situations, I must listen to the voice of Jesus whisper, "Peace—be still!"

Over time, the Apostle Paul learned to put his trust in God in every situation. He was someone who could have meaningfully sung the words Mr. Spafford wrote, that all

166 WALKING IN TRUST

was well with his soul. Paul composed similar lines from prison when he wrote, "I have learned to be content whatever the circumstances" (Philippians 4:12). Peace reigned in Paul's life because Christ reigned in his life. That is the lifestyle I continually seek. Just as Sage learned to trust Greg and me over time and therefore developed more peace in her life, so peace is taking deeper root in my life as I allow myself to trust more in God, allowing his reign instead of fighting his will with my own.

The peace I'm pursuing as I lean more fully on God is like a grain of sand compared with others who face boulder-sized hardships and battles. Christians living in Burma, Indonesia, Cuba, Iran and many other parts of the world, face arrest and even death for their faith (according to both the Christian Solidarity Worldwide and The Voice of the Martyrs, international organizations which monitor Christian persecution around the globe). In November 2011, church leaders in Hanoi, Vietnam were attacked. Men, women, and children were seriously injured during their meeting and the pastor was threatened with death should he continue his preaching. In Nigeria, bombs were detonated on Christmas day 2011 during a Catholic mass, killing nearly forty people. Within days, a militant Islamic group in northern Nigeria issued an ultimatum: Christians were warned to leave the area. In that country and many others, churches are torched and Christians are threatened, injured or killed. I have so much less to fear and bemoan. Those who display peace despite threats, despite torture, despite death, are heroes of the faith. Through fear and persecution, many find peace, just as Spafford wrote in the hymn, "It is Well with My Soul."

Clearly, evil exists in the world. Struggles are not uncommon. And bad things happen to good people: the loss of a job, the end of a relationship, the battle with a major illness, the confrontation of violence, or the waywardness of a child or spouse. Yet, the psalmist says, "Listen to what God the LORD says; he promises peace to his people, his faithful servants." (Psalm 85:8). I have to remind myself to listen to God; not to myself or to the manipulative murmurings in my ear and heart that try to steal my peace. My emotions can cause sea billows to roll in my own life, creating an even greater tidal wave and stealing peace.

My personal applecart was upset when I first found out that Sage was going blind. I was horrified. Many questions ran through my mind. *How can I live with a blind dog? How is she going to get around?* I envisioned getting another dog to be her seeing-eye dog, to help her maneuver the house and the yard. But then I thought, *Why can't I be her eyes and assist her in adapting to her new home?* And that's just what I did.

I had to teach Sage to navigate the stairs in the house and the curbs of the sidewalk. She could not comprehend the empty spaces between the steps. I imagine she thought she was stepping into "nothingness." She flattened herself on the floor and had to be gently yet firmly coaxed to maneuver the stairs. She learned to use her nose as a guide, especially when going up the stairs, by allowing her muzzle to nudge each step.

I placed throw rugs in the living room and dining room. Those tactile items helped her understand the position of household furniture. Her cognitive mapping skills kicked in due to our repetitive route through the neighborhood each day, giving her peace during our daily walks. Not moving the furniture in our home kept her safe and less stressed. Because of all this, Sage became more content, peace-filled and confident as her eyesight diminished, and she developed self-assurance to navigate her world.

One would think Sage would be petrified of navigating

anything unfamiliar. But, there is a peace that passes all understanding, even in a blind dog's world. As the owner of such a dog, I helped Sage develop that peace and confidence. And doing so made me realize how I rely on God's spirit of peace to infiltrate my being so that I can be more peace-filled when life's storms of uncertainty and change thunder over me.

PRAYER:

Lord, you promised peace to your people. Help me to hear your whispered words of peace so that I may be strengthened when storms rock my world and when life's challenges threaten to over-whelm me. Grant me your peace that surpasses all understanding so that I can firmly say, 'It is well with my soul!' Amen.

26
Reliable

Strong God....I can always count on you—God, my dependable love.
—Psalm 59:17, THE MESSAGE

Leaving the office to go home for the day, I reminisce. I've been living in Casper for a few years now, working for an oil company. In a few weeks I'll be leaving this job to begin a new career path as a volunteer and education coordinator. Though I'll miss many of the people I've come to know at this office, most of whom attended Greg's and my wedding, I smile with anticipation of this new chapter in my life.

I turn the key to start my Subaru Impreza. Nothing happens. I try again. Still nothing. It's early April and light snow is falling. It's also after 5:00 p.m. and getting darker by the moment. I try the key again... no connection. I run back into the office and find a few people still there. I go into one of the cubicles, that of a gentleman who graciously helped Greg and me move into our house. Thankfully, Tom is still at work. I tell him my situation, and he follows me outside. He begins checking the engine. He wiggles wires and looks at all those other car parts I know nothing about.

He tries the key—still no luck. Tom then informs me he is sure my battery is dead, so he rushes to get his truck

and bring it close to my car. Then he attaches jumper cables
kept inside his truck and jumpstarts my small red car with
his vehicle. The tactic works. Still, Tom follows me home to
make sure I get there safely.

By this time, Greg is already home from work, so he
and Tom spend time tinkering. As the two men try to
discover the car's problem, I make Sage's dinner. She stands
in the kitchen, waiting for her bowl of kibbles and gravy. She
depends on someone to take care of her. She can't pour the
bag of dog food into her dish. She can't remove her leash
from its hook in the hallway, open the door, and take herself
for a walk. I set Sage's food dish on the floor, then glance
out the window at Greg and Tom, but once again focus
my attention on my dog. All dogs rely upon the kindness
of humans. Those strays that are unfortunate to not have
homes often don't live long; it's difficult to survive on garbage scraps and no shelter from cold and rain. Sage has a
warm house, loving people, and plenty of food and treats ...
but she relies upon me to provide those things.

I'm relying upon Tom and Greg to search for, find, and
fix my car's problem. They eventually discover the cause of
the Subaru's lack of reliability: a tiny, black plastic gizmo has
disconnected from its proper place, and that disconnection
caused the battery to run down. The auto parts store does
not supply that needed piece, so the next morning Greg
orders it from the dealer. By week's end my car has a new
plastic part, a tiny but necessary piece that once again makes
the car dependable enough to drive.

That 1993 vehicle was my first brand-new car. For eighteen
years Michaela, as I christened her, provided the transporta-
tion I needed. Living in West Yellowstone, Montana, for
a few years, I was ninety miles from a major retail store.
Those trips, in addition to traveling through Yellowstone

National Park and the surrounding area for journalism business, racked up the miles. Dependability in a car is paramount when you're a single woman living in an isolated community. Michaela continued serving me consistently through my marriage. Greg and I even drove the car to North Carolina one Christmas to visit family. She ran smoothly and reliably for many years. However, like most elderly things, small health issues became bigger health issues. Even a very small part could create major problems and make for an unreliable vehicle. When the odometer read 265,000 miles, we traded in coughing, clunking Michaela.

Reliability is also important in our relationships with people. A boss needs to know he can count on his employees to show up for work and be productive. Children need to know they can depend on their parents to feed, clothe and care for them. Friends need to know that another friend won't expose a confidence shared in private. The sad story is people aren't always dependable. The good news is, there is One who never fails or disappoints. According to Joshua 1:5, God says, "As I was with Moses, so I will be with you; I will never leave you nor forsake you." We can depend on that.

Sage relied upon me. I fed her. I walked her. I spent time with her. I guided her. I showed Sage my love for her through my dependability. Similarly, God shows us his love through the way he provides for us. He provides employment for Greg and me so we can eat, pay the mortgage and other bills, and care for our pets. And, when I open his Word and offer prayers, his Holy Spirit guides me. I depend upon God for my very existence.

As people and pets age, they depend more upon others for assistance. They need reliable family, friends and caregivers. Sage was not as active in her older years—the days of running through the yard, barking and chasing squirrels gradually came to a close. She no longer spent an entire day outside. As Sage aged, her reliance upon me was greater, and if Greg or I couldn't be home for long periods of time, we asked a neighbor to help us care for her. Cody, our male cocker spaniel, and Sage could no longer wait eight hours to be let outside. Between our dear neighbor and a dependable pet sitter, we ensured that Sage and Cody were cared for, even if Greg and I were gone for long periods of time.

A reliable person is dependable, consistent, and trust-worthy. We are fortunate to have people in our lives who possess these characteristics. Sadly, this isn't always the case. Like me, you have probably experienced the hurt of broken promises and gossiping lips. However, we can rely upon God. He proves trustworthy over and over.

Many people don't believe God is reliable. In the Bible, Mary and Martha at first didn't think Jesus cared when their brother Lazarus died. In fact, Mary questioned him when Jesus showed up three days after Lazarus's death. She said to him, "Lord, if you had been here, my brother would not have died" (John 11:32). But Jesus knew the great miracle he would do and told his disciples how God would be glorified through his tardiness. He says to Lazarus' sisters, "Did I not tell you that if you believed, you would see the glory of God?" (John 11:40). Jesus raised Lazarus from the dead and later, after his own crucifixion, Jesus himself was raised. God doesn't show up too late—he is dependable to do the work needed and answer the prayer spoken.

Abraham's wife, Sarah, became impatient with God and her inability to bear children (see Genesis 15-16). Even though God promised Abraham descendants, Sarah couldn't believe she would become a mother. So, she had her hand-maiden, Hagar, sleep with Abraham. That changed history. The angel told Hagar her son "will be against everyone and everyone's hand against him, and he will live in hostility toward all his brothers" (Genesis 16:12). Though Isaac was born a few years later, fulfilling God's promise to Abraham that he would be the father of many nations, a rift grew between Hagar and Sarah, until Hagar and her son were expelled from Abraham's camp. God, however, did not fail either woman or their sons; he kept his promises to each of them despite the fact that they each tried to take matters into their own hands instead of relying upon God.

There have been times in my own life when I thought God was showing up too late—when I didn't think I could depend upon him. Then I tried to take matters into my own hands; and I made an even bigger mess. In spite of human impatience and inconsistency, though, God remains dependable. He was to Sarah, to Hagar, to Mary and to Lazarus. God is reliable to me as well. When I do follow that pathway of relying upon God, and not upon myself, I display faith and I am blessed. That blessing includes the knowledge that God is always with me as he was with Mary and Sarah.

PRAYER:
Heavenly Father, help me to be more consistent in my actions and words, reflecting your steadfastness. Forgive me of my doubt in your dependability, and help me, through your Holy Spirit, to more firmly rely upon you and not upon myself. Amen.

"My friend, my guide." - Sage with Gayle at a book signing

"Hi, I'm Sage. What's your name?"
Making new friends at a Montana library

27
Trust

Trust in the L<small>ORD</small> with all your heart and lean not on your own understanding; In all your ways, submit to him, and he will direct your paths. –Proverbs 3: 5-6

Our hotel room is on the second floor. I grasp the leash tightly, guiding Sage down the carpeted hallway from the lobby toward the stairway. She walks beside me, putting her nose to the floor occasionally as if to catch a whiff of something familiar. However, there is nothing recognizable about this hotel located in a large town three hundred miles from our home. Still, she walks without hesitation, trusting the one who holds her leash and guides her.

At the stairway I give the command, "Step up!" while tugging the leash slightly forward. Sage places one black-and-white paw upward onto the first step and then continues up seven steps to the landing and another seven steps to the next floor as she follows my commands and my guidance with the leash. Not once does she stumble or hesitate—a testament to how far she has come since she first attempted to climb stairs in a strange building. Through the years of consistent training and quality time together, Sage has learned to trust me to guide her, not only on stairs, but also in life. She understands that I will not purposely let harm come to her.

It's one thing for a blind dog to trust its owners; strangers can be, and sometimes are, another story. Yet, Sage trusted people. Her comfort level around humans proved to be very useful and important. For example, going to the groomer could easily have been a frightening experience for Sage. Being blind since the age of three and deaf in her eleventh year caused her to rely upon the kindness and goodness of people. Sage knew three groomers while living at our house, and all three commented on her calmness and ease. Despite being sprayed with water, lathered up with shampoo, sheared from head to tail, dried loudly with a large hair dryer—often sharing the same large room with dogs and people who were strangers to her—Sage didn't fight or even whimper. She didn't cry or cower. She stayed calm and allowed the person to complete the grooming process. Although she could not see who was clipping her nails, bathing or cutting her hair, she trusted the one wielding the tools.

After Sage received her haircut, she looked stunning. Her sleek, soft, shortened coat not only provided her greater comfort in the summer heat, but also took some weight off her body. Sage became more energetic, her step quickened during our morning walks, and she pranced down the sidewalk. She seemed to know she was beautiful. She acted younger and more graceful. That trust she exhibited with the groomers despite being unable to see them resulted in Sage not only being cleaner and neat, but feeling and acting beautiful.

When I go to my groomer (hair stylist), I don't necessarily prance out the door and dance down the sidewalk as did my blind dog. Although a weight may be lifted from my head in the form of a haircut, weight can only be lifted from my heart when I trust my Creator to guide my life. Jesus said, "I am the true vine, and my Father is the gardener. He cuts off every branch in me that bears no fruit, while every branch that does bear fruit he prunes so that it will be even more fruitful" (John 15:1-2). God, the Divine Gardner and Great Groomer, snips and prunes me, shearing away the unhealthy and unproductive parts of my life. It may be for my good, but I don't enjoy it. Sometimes the shearing is too close to the scalp, too close to the ears, too close to the heart. Just as I have to trust the stylist who cuts my hair, I also need to trust the One who prunes my heart and life. By his love and mercy he makes a beautiful new creation, as God intended. "Therefore, if anyone is in Christ, the new creation has come: The old has gone, the new is here!" (2 Corinthians 5:17).

When my husband prunes our trees, sometimes the end result is not the most beautiful, even if it is necessary. The trees can look ugly without all their branches—and they had no choice in the matter! However, when they rebound from their dormancy, producing even longer, stronger branches and greener, more healthy leaves, the trees become more beautiful, strong and fruitful than they were before the pruning. I have sometimes questioned my husband's trimming of branches only to later see the reasoning behind his act of taking so much off. I have since learned to trust his judgment about trimming trees!

When the woman with the bleeding disorder earnestly sought a healing touch from Jesus, he asked, "Who touched me?" When she confessed, he told her, "Daughter, your faith has healed you. Go in peace and be freed from your suffering" (Mark 5:31-34). Jesus made her even more beautiful and whole because she believed in what he could do; she trusted him. To be made beautiful by the Lord, I also need to trust him—just as Sage trusted those who diligently and lovingly worked to make her beautiful at the doggie salon. When I trust God, whom I can't see, I grow in my faith walk.

David knew first-hand about trusting God, even from

the days before he was king. David tended his father's flocks as a boy and defended them against lions and bears. David faced Goliath but he did it with the Lord at his side. David fled Saul's wrath and, later in life, the pursuit of his own son. David trusted God with his life, his future, and his responsibilities. "When I am afraid, I put my trust in you," he writes in Psalm 56:3. David learned the best place to put his trust was not necessarily in friends, family, or even in himself—but in God.

Sage's trust in me and in Greg did not come right away. She often shied away from our bidding when going for walks in the neighborhood where we first lived—and later, in the new neighborhood. The sound of cars whizzing by, the noise of children playing in the park, and the scent of other dogs along the trail made her nervous. Her lack of sight and her lack of trust in her new guardians could have prevented Sage from enjoying morning and evening strolls. However, persistence on our part and Sage's growing reliance upon us, and not upon herself, as well as her increasing trust in our caregiving, broke through the wall of trepidation, so that when we moved to the new house and neighborhood, she hesitated only slightly when we ventured on that initial walk through the area.

When Sage became deaf in 2010, her anxiety returned. But again, our persistence paid off, and Sage enjoyed walks around the block and through the forest when we visited our cabin with her.

Scripture instructs me to trust in God's guidance. Without him, my soul would wilt and die like a plant without water. "Can papyrus grow tall where there is no marsh? Can reeds thrive without water? While still growing and uncut, they wither more quickly than grass. Such is the destiny of all who forget God" (Job 8:11-13). Papyrus is a tall reed that originally grew along the marshes of the Nile River in

Egypt. The plant could be used for many purposes, and was often made into a type of paper on which to write. Once common during ancient times, this plant, like many species around the world, is rare today. Trust is also becoming an endangered species in people's lives. My trust of others has lessened over the years. People gossip and deceive; airline companies delay and cancel flights; insurance and credit card companies create too much red tape and fine print. With each instance where trust is broken, like the rare papyrus struggling to survive, I become more cynical about what and who to believe. Trust becomes fragile and skepticism grows.

I do trust in many things, often without realizing it: from pilots flying me forty-thousand feet above the earth, to the lowly seat of my dining room chair. That airplane weighs thousands of pounds and still smoothly glides above the clouds. That chair takes the weight of my body and doesn't collapse from underneath me (although at times I am sure I feel it quiver!). Who gave people the wisdom, knowledge and ability to create such things, to defy gravity and weight, to rise above the clouds? I am often amazed at the ingenuity and capability of people; yet I also know Who is the giver of all wisdom and knowledge. Medicine is a prime example. I trust my physician and veterinarian to correctly diagnose illness and prescribe the right medicine. Who has provided them with the wisdom and discernment as well as the invention of equipment and development of medications? The answer is God—the One I cannot see. He is the One I can truly believe in and rely upon. "For the LORD gives wisdom; from his mouth come knowledge and understanding" (Proverbs 2:6).

Just as Sage unwaveringly placed her trust in me, in her groomer and her veterinarian—all whom she could not see and could no longer hear—so, too, can I place my trust in God, whom I can neither see nor hear. He grooms me, he prunes me, and he cares for me. His Word reassures me, his provision supplies me, and his blessings surround me. God's word is his bond, as the psalmist declares. "The works of his hands are faithful and just; all his precepts are trustworthy. They are established forever and ever, enacted in faithfulness and uprightness" (Psalm 111: 6-8).

PRAYER:
Lord, help me to remember that your promises cannot be broken, and that I can trust you in all things—even when the shearing tool is sharp. As you are trustworthy, help me to be more trust-worthy in what you have provided: family, friends, job, posses-sions. I thank you for your promises and your blessings. Amen.

28
Rest

By the seventh day God had finished the work he had been doing;
so on the seventh day he rested from all his work. And God blessed
the seventh day and made it holy, because on it he rested from all
the work of creating that he had done. —Genesis 2:2-3

The television blares with sirens and shootings. A marathon
of my favorite TV program airs this particular Saturday, and
I am hunkered down for the evening. Sitting in my recliner
with Sage beside me, I welcome the diversion. The day has
been full, and I am weary. Sage seems to understand that I
need this "down time"; she wiggles closer, stretching her body
as far as the tipped-back chair allows. The Audubon clock in
the sunroom chirps like a sparrow, so it's eight o'clock. I have
been awake since before six this morning, doing housework.
A Chinook wind ushers in a reprieve from March snow and
cold. I had filled my day with spring cleaning, beginning
with scrubbing floors and opening windows to air out the
winter blahs. Now, night falls and winter's chill sets in again.
Greg stokes the woodstove and heads for his home office
downstairs, leaving me to relish warmth from the fire and the
dog cuddling next to me. Wrapping myself with my favorite
crocheted afghan, I allow rest to take root.

Saturdays are typically my work-around-the-house days. My mother raised me that way, doing laundry, dusting, and vacuuming indoors, and mowing and weeding outdoors. When you work full time outside the home, Saturdays are often the best days to accomplish such tasks.

Closet cleaning is one chore that doesn't get done regularly at my house. On that particular Saturday in mid March, I decided to launch into that project as well as many others. In addition to cleaning the bedroom and bathroom closets, my "to do" list included organizing kitchen drawers and mopping floors. I also planned to plant some indoor herbs. My laundry loads included heavy items like quilts. The day was pleasant, so I opened several windows to let in the early springtime breeze and warmth. That's when it dawned on me that we had lived in this house for nearly three years without one window having been washed. Another chore added to the list!

Although only Greg and I and the pets live in this house with more than eighteen hundred square feet, the size is double what our rental house was. The two bathrooms need to be cleaned regularly. We also have dog beds and cat-litter boxes. Greg often washes dishes and makes meals. He usually takes out the trash, too. But unless asked, he's not one to jump right in and clean the house—especially when his wife decides it's time for spring cleaning! I arose before six that morning, and by six o'clock that night, no windows had been washed and no herbs had been planted. I had only cleaned out my own clothes closet and one bathroom closet, both of which hadn't been cleared out and organized in the three years since we moved into the house (I decided then that my husband would have to tackle the chore of organizing his own clothes, no matter how disorderly his closet became!).

Then, after numerous loads of laundry, I tackled

reorganizing the kitchen cabinets and rearranged my home office. That evening I vowed to one day be like my friend Lesley and hire out house cleaning chores!

My dear husband stayed out of my way all day, deciding the garage needed a spruce up as well. Yet he also threw some burgers on the grill, for which I was grateful; I was also tired. No, I was exhausted!

Though I had good intentions of washing windows the next week, winter returned to our community—and the windows never did get washed that year.

Being industrious is part of my DNA. I believe that God desires his people to work and to work diligently. God himself did the work of creating the world; and he even gave chores to the first person he created. "The LORD God took the man and put him in the Garden of Eden to work it and take care of it," records Genesis 2:15. But God rested after his six days of work, and he expects people to rest also. In the book of Exodus, the Lord tells the Israelites, "Six days you shall labor and do all your work, but the seventh day is a Sabbath to the LORD your God. On it you shall not do any work, neither you, nor your son or daughter, nor your man servant or maid servant, nor your animals, nor the alien within your gates" (Exodus 20:9-10). God knows the value of work and he knows the value of rest.

Jesus, too, knew the importance of rest. When Jesus and his disciples traveled, crowds numbering into the thousands often overwhelmed them. Mark records in his Gospel, "Then, because so many people were coming and going that they did not even have a chance to eat, [Jesus] said to [his disciples], 'Come with me by yourselves to a quiet place and get some rest'" (Mark 6:31). Although work is necessary, rest is critical. Jesus understood these principles. How often do I push myself to warp speed but then crash and burn? How much better I would feel emotionally and physically if I took more time to slow down and rest! How often do I quiet myself, and enjoy a Sabbath rest? Thankfully, I do more now than I used to.

There are still days when I act like a rabbit on steroids. I have a tendency to push myself beyond what my body or spirit can handle. Instead of working nearly nonstop those twelve hours in March, I probably should have worked eight or ten and saved the other chores for a few different evenings. I didn't accomplish all I wanted to anyway. The herb planting didn't get done until a different day. The windows ... well, they are still waiting!

Jesus rested and prayed, knowing that time to commune with his heavenly Father was vital. Jesus understood the importance of quiet time and prayer. He knew the significance of rest.

Sage, too, knew the value of rest. Although we took walks and she spent time in the backyard, she spent many hours sleeping, especially as an older dog. Even when she was younger, though, after games of tag with the cats and a rousing game of catch-me-if-you-can with the backyard squirrels, Sage found a comfortable place to nap. Back then, her favorite spots to sleep were a perfectly-dug "nest" near the house or the couch inside our home. Later she slumbered on dog blankets and rugs inside the house or on the living-room recliner with me. Perhaps Sage understood her aging body could not do what it used to do, and took care of it by resting. I am wise to follow her example!

I was raised by very hard-working parents who didn't always observe the Sabbath, although they tried to do very little actual work on Sundays. My mother was a stay-at-home mom for a number of reasons through my teenage years. That did not mean she sat on the couch watching soap operas and eating bon bons. While I was at school, she cleaned house and cooked. She also took care of livestock and other animals on our small farm and planted and tended a large garden. She painted the house inside and out and she helped my dad with a variety of home and farm projects. She also visited and helped neighbors and attended school functions like PTA meetings and parent-teacher conferences. She was raised on a farm and knew the labor involved in keeping even a small acreage productive and her family fed.

My mother exhibited many of the qualities of the Proverbs 31 woman: "She selects wool and flax and works with eager hands… She sets about her work vigorously; her arms are strong for her tasks" (Proverbs 31:13-17). To this day, mom doesn't watch soaps or eat bon bons. She does, however, enjoy a baseball game on TV now and again. And, more importantly, she knows when to rest. She never did set aside a specific day of rest, but she does rest when her body, mind and spirit call her to do so; for she has wisely come to understand that over exertion is damaging to one's body and spirit.

My husband is also an industrious worker. Since I met him more than twelve years ago, he has embodied the entrepreneurial spirit. He worked for a television station as a news photographer while simultaneously developing his own video business. After our marriage he took the leap of faith and left the TV station to operate his own business full time. Although money can get tight, he continues exploring new options for the business. He examines avenues to diversify and educates himself on cutting edge technology. He also explores new marketing techniques and weighs partnership options. There are weeks when he works from six in the morning until midnight, juggling the various aspects of his entrepreneurial path. Though his heart and body know he can't maintain such a pace seven days a week, there are times when he has done that because he is compelled to take care of us and is driven to not give up—even in the toughest of economic times. Yet, I often scold him for doing too much. I try to encourage him to rest, to go fishing where he can relax beside a mountain stream, or simply to sit in his chair and watch his favorite baseball or basketball team. Sometimes he listens; but mostly he maintains his fast pace. When he listens to his own spiritual and bodily rhythms and finally does take a break, he feels renewed both emotionally and physically. He, too, knows rest is important, but his inner clock differs drastically from mine, and I've learned to respect that.

The Bible advises us to work and to work hard. "He who works his land will have abundant food, but he who chases fantasies lacks judgment," states Proverbs 12:11. In other words, no soap operas and bon-bons! Working is not only for our good, but also for the good of others, so that we can share with those who struggle more than we do. Paul instructs believers to not embrace idleness (1 Thessalonians 3:6-15).

A synonym for *idleness* is *laziness*. The word *lazy* brings to mind the picture of a bloodhound lounging on a cabin porch. But dogs are not really lazy (well, elderly dogs sleep a lot, but they also still enjoy their walks and squirrel chasings!). Bloodhounds are often used as search dogs because of their keen sense of smell. Search-and-rescue dogs and service dogs have endless energy for their many duties. Those dogs that searched for bodies after the 9/11 attacks worked long hours—search handlers have said these dogs didn't want to quit. However, rest became vital for their emotional and physical well being, as well as that of their handlers. Rest is critical for both man and beast.

Sage was less active by the time she was five years old. Even walks became more leisurely. Just like my mother, who cannot do at age seventy what she did at age fifty, and I cannot do at age fifty what I did at age twenty-five, Sage did not engage in as much physical activity as when she was younger. Aging takes its toll, even on our pets. Sage wasn't lazy; neither am I. There is just less energy! After a very full day of nine or ten hours at work, or spending ten or twelve hours cleaning house, I need downtime. Following Sage's example, and the example of both my mother and my Lord, I have learned to rest.

As I read Proverbs 31, I see to what I can aspire and to where I often fall short. Though I cannot be that Proverbs 31 woman this side of heaven, God loves me anyway … and thankfully, so does my husband. I am not a robot nor am I a rabbit on batteries that can go on and on and on. I am expected to work, yes, as one of the household bread winners and as a Christian. However, I am also called to rest. When my spirit as well as my body is weary, Jesus does not condemn me. He says, "Come to me all you who are weary and burdened, and I will give you rest. Take my yoke upon you and learn from me … and you will find rest for your souls" (Matthew 11:28-29). He invites me to lay my tiredness and anxious burdens at his nail-scarred feet and to rest my head on his loving shoulder.

Within the word *restore* is the word *rest*. God restores my soul when I rest. I desire God's restoration; but to accomplish that, I need to spend time and be still with him so he can breathe that Sabbath restoration within me.

Restoration is the name of God's game—restoration for Israel and restoration for the followers of Jesus. From their captivity in Egypt and later in Babylon to the restoration by the coming of the Messiah, God desires restoration for his people.

When Sage was a younger dog, specially-made dog beds had no appeal to her. She liked my bed and would easily jump up on it to spend her day in comfort while I was at work. Even though she couldn't see where she was jump-ing, she had done it enough times to land on the bed instead of the floor. She didn't always spend her days in bed,

though. During warm-season days, she stayed outdoors in
our fenced-in backyard. She enjoyed sniffing and exploring.
Or, if she stayed indoors while I was at work, I'd leave her
with a chew toy filled with treats. The scent attracted her
spaniel nose and kept her interested and occupied. Additionally, she and I would walk the neighborhood both morning
and evening to give us both some exercise. Some days we'd
also play games of tug-of-war.

In her later years, however, arthritis limited her jumping,
and doggie beds on the floor were more comfortable for her.
The toys were packed away and walks were limited to going
around the block. Squirrels got chased only a few times each
week during the nicer weather. I can't help but think that if
Proverbs 31 had been written about dogs, Sage would have
failed as miserably as I when I compare myself with this
"wonder woman." Yet, God has loved us both despite our
limitations.

As I wait for the day when all of God's creation will
be completely restored, I will strive to do the work he sets
before me. I will also choose to rest and be restored by him. I
may not be the perfect Proverbs 31 woman, but I can honor
the Lord with the work he's given me, both in and out of the
home. When I honor him in my labor and in my rest, I find
satisfaction; I also may find I do fulfill some of the facets of
Proverbs 31: "Give her the reward she has earned, and let her
works bring her praise at the city gate" (verse 31).

PRAYER:
*Heavenly Father, may I honor you with my work, but may I
also remember to spend time at rest, in quiet with you. Through
that rest, restore me through the power of your Holy Spirit, that
I may do the work to which you've called me. In Jesus' name I
pray. Amen.*

29
Gratitude

Let the word of Christ dwell in you richly as you teach and admonish one another with all wisdom as you sing psalms, hymns, and spiritual songs with gratitude in your hearts to God.
—Colossians 3:16

This quiet morning I gaze with satisfaction at our newly-finished cabin. My coffee is brewing in the galley-style kitchen. Mid-September has arrived; our twelve-by-forty cabin has been set on its foundation on our mountain property before the winter season hits. Greg and I have spent the past several days cleaning and furnishing the place. Although we bought the "Park" model cabin nearly two years ago, our work to thin out the lodgepole pine trees and to save for the cost of a foundation has taken not only energy but also time. Now, a week after erecting the cabin, we are installing a stronger roof to help mitigate the heavy winter snow. A small chocolate-colored woodstove gleams in the corner of the living room, awaiting its first fire. My parents are visiting, eager to see our new "summer home on wheels"—though the wheels have been removed per county regulations so the cabin can set permanently on a concrete base.

While Greg, Mom and Dad sleep in, I go out to the screened porch and situate myself in one of the wicker chairs. I sip my cup of hot coffee, basking in the beauty and solitude of the pine forest and the freshness of the sun rising on a new day.

My ears try to pick up the usual sounds. But all I hear is … quiet. No car horns, no traffic noise, no television blaring—not even a telephone ringing. Wanting our mountain retreat to be a serene escape from daily activities, Greg and I chose a property with limited electricity. Three solar panels provide us with lights that Greg installed just last weekend. We use a camp cooler for storing cold food, and a propane stove for cooking. Our neighbors are the mule deer and songbirds that reside on the mountain. Squirrels prevail in the trees around the cabin, and we can occasionally hear them chatter. Other nature noises include the breeze in the trees and the remnant of hummingbirds that zip around the last of the year's yellow daisies.

Before my family rises for the day, I treasure this alone time with creation and the great Creator. I silently count my blessings: this special place of solitude; my two dogs, sleeping silently on the blue braided rug placed on the porch just for them; dear parents who are able to come for a visit; and a loving husband who worked so diligently with me to create this haven. How many times have I taken these gifts for granted? I whisper a word of thanksgiving.

I open my Bible and read Psalm 103, giving praise to my Lord who forgives and heals, who redeems and loves, and who satisfies my desires with good things. I am reminded that God has granted not only things I can see, but also benefits that I cannot see. God's love and grace are also special gifts—with eternal benefits. My mind then recalls the crucifixion scene from the movie *The Passion of the Christ*, and I again imagine the cost of that love and forgiveness.

Thanksgiving wells up in my heart and, like Old Faithful geyser, gratitude engulfs my soul. I raise my hands and whisper my praise. Tears spill from my eyes.

The words of "The Doxology," written in 1674 by Thomas Ken, ring in my heart: "Praise God from whom all blessings flow; Praise him all creatures here below," and I whisper those in worship to the Lord. I sit in silence for a few more moments, relishing this quiet time.

Footsteps pad down the short hallway of the cabin; I glance in that direction. The dogs sense another presence as well. They raise their heads from the warm rug and turn toward the sound. I rise from my chair to greet my approaching visitor. The smell of coffee has awakened my mother, and she joins me on the wooden porch. We smile and embrace. I walk to the kitchen to pour her a cup of steaming coffee, and as I return to the porch, she points down our dirt driveway. Four wild turkeys stand there, seemingly perplexed about this structure now standing where just a few days before there were only dirt and pines. In the five years of owning this parcel of land, turkeys never appeared on the property—at least, not in our presence. We had heard them a few years ago and had observed some about two miles down the main mountain road; but this particular morning, a week after setting up our little mountain home, here they are!

In quiet wonder Mom and I watch the turkeys amble toward the cabin. We stay silent; so they come closer. Now Cody, the cocker spaniel, smells and sees them. He stands on a chair, front paws at the window screen, stretching as long as his little spaniel body allows. Then he happily welcomes the creatures in his own way: *"Whoof! Whoof, Whoof!"* The birds do a quick turkey trot through the woods and disappear. Mom and I laugh. My heart again whispers a quiet praise to my Lord and his tremendous blessings this September morning.

The early American colonists at Plymouth enjoyed a harvest in thankfulness in 1621, sharing bounty with their Native American neighbors. However, it was not until 1863, when President Abraham Lincoln proclaimed a national Thanksgiving Day, that this country honored a special day of gratitude. Today, the fourth Thursday in November is recognized as a national day of thanksgiving, and all across the country people gather with family and friends or to serve a meal to those in need. This day helps Americans reflect upon their bounty and blessings. As Christians, we know from where those blessings come.

Should we give thanks just one day of the year? Scripture tells us that our lives should be lived in thanksgiving. "Let us come before him with thanksgiving and extol him with music and song" (Psalm 95:2). New Testament writers also encourage God's people to live a life of thanksgiving. Paul's letter to the Colossians is filled with exhortations to give thanks. "Devote yourselves to prayer, being watchful and thankful," he writes in Colossians 4:2.

Giving thanks to God can be quite easy when life is going smoothly. Praising him for safety and provision isn't hard. But when life is challenging it becomes more difficult for me to be thankful. Like Jacob in the Old Testament, I wrestle with God, not wanting to give thanks during my struggles. When the pets suddenly become ill and the vet bills need payment, or when our two cars break down simultaneously, those tangible troubles give rise to discouragement.

The Apostle Paul reminds us that these times are temporary and that we should focus on an eternal glory. He encourages us to not lose heart, but instead to "fix our eyes not on what is seen, but on what is unseen. For what is seen is temporary, but what is unseen is eternal" (2 Corinthians 4:18). That is something to be thankful for—that this life and its problems are temporary and that the great hope I look forward to is eternal. I am also encouraged when I recall God's blessings of times past. Being mindful of what he's done before helps me deal with what goes on in the present.

I am reminded often to focus more on the small blessings. When I go to the laundry room, for example, I whisper a word of thanks for that machine. I've been without a washing machine in times past, including when my fourteen-year-old machine finally gave up the ghost. Not having that convenience is a major pain, especially when one has dog and people blankets to wash! I once worked for a visitor center that taught about western history. I learned a great deal about those pioneers who rode in wagons or walked for six months, about the chore of washing dishes and clothes in a river, or the times when they couldn't wash clothes or themselves for days! How thankful I am to live today with showers and tubs, dishwashers and washing machines! My grandmothers didn't even have those conveniences.

When Greg and I go to the cabin, I gain a little understanding of what those pioneers and my own grandmothers dealt with. With no refrigerator and no piped water, I use things more sparingly. We bring water from our house in town and I take the used dishes from the cabin home to wash. Paper plates are a convenience we use when we're staying more than a day or two, and though I don't like accumulating so much trash, I'm grateful someone invented such an item for those days we need them. It might seem trivial, but that gratitude is genuine … if sometimes forgotten.

God's people are not a perfect people. I am far from perfect. I let the Lord down again and again. His chosen people, the Israelites, acted similarly. After God freed them from Pharaoh in Egypt, the people grumbled about this and that and erected idols to worship. Even though he provided for them in the desert and eventually brought them to the Promised Land, they continued to stray from him. Then they became captives of Babylon. Yet through the prophet Jeremiah, God promised restoration.

God's grace in providing restoration gives me great reason for gratitude. The fact that I can worship freely also gives me good reason. I am thankful to live in America. Despite the countless problems and uncertainties this country faces, I believe I am greatly blessed to have freedoms the vast majority of people in the world do not have. I can attend church or a Bible study and not fear imprisonment or death. I attend Christian concerts out in the open—even in a park—without danger or persecution. The apostles, those first Christ followers, faced fears of imprisonment or worse, and many were martyred for their faith. I am thankful for the freedoms I still enjoy.

Sage enjoyed many things in life, too. Walking through the woods near our cabin, for example, allowed her to investigate numerous scents she could not pick up in our city neighborhood. Sage's tail wagging demonstrated her thanksgiving for the walks and the woodland smells. Her vocalized *Awhoo! Awhoo!* spoke of the gratitude she had when I came home from work and filled her food dish. Her flag tail beat against the floor when I petted her, expressing her pleasure and gratitude. When she nuzzled next to me and laid her long black muzzle on my lap, I knew she was thankful.

I have wondered on more than one occasion what might have happened to Sage if Greg and I had not adopted her, and the possibilities are chilling to me. I am thankful that God prompted Greg to insist that we adopt her. God used this incredible dog to teach me many life lessons, and to share those lessons with others. God can use anyone and anything for the purpose of instruction. He speaks and teaches in ways he knows will touch the hearts of his people.

For me, that often comes through creation, including his creation of a springer spaniel named Sage. I am grateful to God for the gift of a dog's companionship on this earthly journey. He has blessed me several times with a canine friend, but none touched my heart and impacted my life as much as Sage. I will forever be thankful to the Lord for the unique and beautiful gift of Sage!

PRAYER:

Dear Lord, I am grateful to you for how you speak to my heart, and for the multitude of blessings that you have bestowed upon me. Forgive me when I take your blessings for granted. Help me to have a more thankful heart. Amen.

30
Perseverance

Let us run with perseverance the race marked out for us.
–Hebrews 12:1

The autumn day dawns clear. A white, full moon hovers brightly against the slate-gray sky. I spend twenty minutes in quiet with the Lord then close my Bible with satisfaction and anticipation of the day. My list of to-dos is extensive, yet do-able, and I approach the day planning to hit a home run. But, like a baseball player over-reaching the bat, I swing at the day and miss the mark.

The morning progresses, and as it does I struggle with my to-do list as a series of interruptions are hurled at me like fastballs from a pitcher. My two dogs aren't acting like senior pets. Instead of lying quietly, they pace. So I put them in the backyard. Just as I start to relax and get productive, they begin a barkfest competition with the neighbor dogs, forcing me to bring them back inside. No sooner do they come in than they are once again whining at the backdoor. They want to be outside in the yard to bask in the pleasant September warmth and have earnest "conversation" with their four-footed neighbors. After several minutes of listening to their begging, I relent. Out they go.

Strike One!

The next play transpires when a cranky phone technician arrives at my home. A new phone line needs to be installed, and he doesn't appear happy about the task. He sulks. He slams the back door, his tool kit, and even the wooden gate to the backyard. Customer service doesn't seem to be his primary objective today! Oh, and did I mention that the dogs aren't thrilled with him either? You guessed it—more barking!

Strike Two!

I try to focus on my computer work, attempting to accomplish the writing goals I set for myself earlier in the day: complete a semi-monthly gardening e-newsletter and compose a nature article about sandhill crane migration and how those birds can inspire us to persevere. But the computer refuses to cooperate. The newsletter won't format correctly, the cursor doesn't stay in its proper place, and the Internet isn't running smoothly.

Glitch.
Kicked out.
Freeze.
Reboot and restart.
Begin again.
Glitch.
Kicked out.
Freeze.
Reboot and restart.
Begin again.
Repeat.
Strike Three!
And four, and five!

There may be only three strikes for an "out" in baseball, but I am up to nearly a half-dozen. Somewhere between a simmer and boil, I lose my cool. Instead of persevering like the large-winged sandhill cranes I researched and wrote about, my fists clench, my face scrunches, and my mind and heart conduct a primordial scream.

Those trying days—times of little irritants and hours of major roadblocks—come out of nowhere. They can twist their way into my spirit like a flat-headed bolt digging into wood. Demands and annoyances jab me like barbed grass. That's when I need to be like the cranes that regularly preen themselves and continue on their flight journey—I, too, need to pluck the barbs from my spirit and persevere through obstacles, not primal scream at them.

Perseverance is the name of the game on this earth, and, like baseball, it's a game I don't naturally play well. I need help. My coach is God. His Holy Spirit and his holy Word provide the assistance I need to persevere in this life. Paul says in 1 Corinthians 9:24, "Do you know that in a race all the runners run, but only one gets the prize? Run in such a way as to get the prize." Running marathons or even jogging through town are not skills I gainfully employ … or even care to try. But life is a race that, if I run it properly, yields great reward. James 1:12 tells me, "Blessed is the one who perseveres under trial because, having stood the test, that person will receive the crown of life that the Lord has promised to those who love him."

Sage needed perseverance to travel the journey of her life; I also have needed an enduring spirit. Being blind is a challenge for both dog and owner. Yet, we set our minds to meet those challenges. The routine passes through the house and neighborhood and the training of new commands took patience and endurance. Our trips to the vet's office and the travels to schools and libraries took persistence. The walks in the woods and Sage being lost in the forest all took courage and perseverance. Both Sage and I chose to persevere through this darkened path, meeting each challenge as it came, and walking in trust with one another and our Creator.

Perseverance and trust would be deeply challenged in the later season of Sage's life. In September 2010, she became deaf. The loss was gradual, much like her sight had diminished slowly ten years previous. However, deafness affected Sage's attitude for several days. She stopped eating and became listless. We coddled her, even attempting to feed her from our hands. Sage lost interest in walking, and she appeared more confused when trying to maneuver around the house. Hearing, one of her most acute senses and the one she heavily relied upon after losing her sight, was now silent. Like Helen Keller of years ago, my dear dog withdrew from the world. For both Sage and me, discouragement set in like poured concrete. We silently suffered in unison.

Since Sage could no longer respond to our voices, Greg and I needed to find a way to communicate with her differently. We tried high-pitched whistles, but she gave no response. We decided to tune into her remaining few senses. Since her hearing could no longer serve as her homing device, I set up incense sticks and wax warmers in various rooms of the house, enticing her sense of smell. Touch also became a higher priority, and we practiced numerous simple ideas. We could not use sign language in Sage's paw like Helen Keller's teacher signed into her hand, but we discovered other ways of touch to communicate with Sage. For example, whenever we were in the same room with her, we gently touched the top of her head to let her know we were close by. We also guided her with a gentle tug to her collar. Sage was an intelligent dog, and she mastered this new form of communication quickly. Her response to life returned, although the vigor and vitality she once exhibited became muted along with her hearing.

Just when we thought we had answered this challenge, on the heels of deafness came another test. In the spring of

2011, as I prepared for work, Greg called my name. Fear
resonated in his voice, and I trotted into the living room
where I found him on the floor, kneeling beside Sage. Her
elongated body was quivering and her blind, gray eyes had
rolled back into her head. Greg looked at me in trepidation.

"Something's really wrong," he said hoarsely.

We rushed Sage to the vet, and after his examination
Dr. Johnson informed us Sage would have to be hospitalized
for at least a day, possibly longer. He explained that she had
experienced something like a stroke, a condition known as
vestibular syndrome.

Sage recovered, but almost exactly one month later, she
experienced another seizure. Again, she recovered. However,
less than a year later, more than eleven years after we
adopted her, Greg and I bid farewell to our sweet Sage, the
amazing dog who so wonderfully touched our lives—and
the lives of hundreds, perhaps thousands, of other people.
The silent invader, cancer, permeated her internal organs,
unbeknownst to us until the final week of her life. As Dr.
Johnson gently inserted the needle to alleviate her suffering,
we kissed her and talked with her. Sage's heart slowed then
ceased, and her spirit left us for her eternal reward. There
were no dry eyes in the room that morning, for Sage's sweetness and courage had left a tender paw print on the hearts of
her vet and his staff as well.

Sage persevered even through the cancer, not succumb-
ing to the deadly attack until the last week of her life.
She and I had visited friends just a short time previous,
walking their ranch amidst the wild turkeys, mule deer, and
songbirds as well as visiting the llamas, horses, and cattle in
the fields. Sage's tail wagged and her nose sniffed; she gave
no indication of a significant illness. My blind dog's tenacity
was apparent to all of us from the day Dr. Johnson diagnosed
her with Progressive Retinal Atrophy in 2001 to the day

he helped her cross from her earthly life to her heavenly reward eleven years later. Sage completed her calling as our companion and friend; she completed the race, as the Apostle Paul mentions in Scripture, and she completed it with courageous perseverance.

In between Sage's seizures and her death, Cody, our cocker spaniel, also experienced major health issues. He was ultimately diagnosed with an autoimmune disorder. His four-day stay at the hospital added to our significant vet bill. Simultaneously, the Toyota Matrix we owned went through a period of repair needs, and our ten-year-old washing machine found a home in the local dump. Six weeks later, just as Cody was slowly climbing back from the autoimmune setback, he tore his left ACL, one of the ligaments in his knee.

The old Batman TV show often displayed this comic-script text during fight scenes: *Bam! Pow! Bam!* Those words jumped from the screen into my reality; I felt sucker-punched, like a two-by-four slamming into my body multiple times in a gauntlet. As those gut-punches transpired, my perseverance level dropped off the radar. My heart echoed the bemoaning of Job when he lamented, "I loathe my very life; therefore I will give free rein to my compliant and speak out in the bitterness of my soul. I say to God: Do not declare me guilty, but tell me what charges you have against me" (Job 10: 1-2). Though I felt I was being punished running this gauntlet-style race, the Apostle James says I should consider it joy whenever I face many trials because when my faith is tested, it will produce perseverance (see James 1:2-3). It's hard to find joy when you're running a thicket of heart-piercing propor-tions. But there is a goal when one goes through such a stinging skirmish: to simply get through it!

When turmoils taunt me and I'm running the emotional gauntlet, I often dash to our special place in the mountains. During that late summer, after Cody tore his ACL and was

receiving treatment for the autoimmune disease, I decided
it was time to run. In addition to the assault on Cody's
health and the stockpile of vet bills and the car and washing
machine woes, a friend had unexpectedly died. So, I took
an early morning trip to our cabin with Sage. Located only
twenty minutes from our house, this property has become
my sanctuary. It is here where I feel closest to God, surrounded by the solitude and solace of his creation.

I left Sage in the cabin with her blanket and chew stick
and walked through the pine forest. I paused now and again
to gaze at the lofty lodgepole pines and wipe the tears
of weariness and despair from my eyes. The late August
warmth enveloped the thickly-wooded mountainscape, but
my heart felt raw and chilled, like a Rocky Mountain January. Even under the bright summer sky, winter's gloom satu-
rated my heart.

Fists clenched in frustration, I wove between standing
trees and downed timber and kicked dirt clods. Tears freely
flowing, I cried to the Lord the word many people utter
when they suffer emotional distress: *Why?* Many times in
my life I have pleaded with the Lord to change my circumstances, and here I was again! Most times, however, he
doesn't change the situation; instead, he looks to change me
and my response. Through this race of life, gauntlet that it
can be, God wants me to persevere. As Paul says in Romans
5:4, "perseverance produces character and character produces
hope"; hope is what one needs in times of trouble. During
such times of distress, it's easy to think I'm the only one
suffering, but Scripture says nothing overtakes me that is
uncommon to others (1 Corinthians 10:13). Even Jesus was
tempted. He called out to his Heavenly Father prior to
his crucifixion to "take this cup from me" (Mark 14:36).
The Apostle Paul asked God to remove the "thorn in his
flesh" (2 Corinthians 12:7-8). God did not change either

circumstance. Both men persevered, Jesus all the way to the cross, giving up his own life for me, the apostles, and millions of other people.

As I strolled the pine-covered property, more words from the Bible came to mind. I recalled a recent sermon by our pastor about putting on the armor of God (see Ephesians 6:11-17). The sword of the Spirit is the Word of God; Scripture is my weapon when the enemy seeks to destroy me through my trials and even my thoughts. I began to recite Bible verses, remembering that my battles are not against flesh and blood but against the dark powers of this world and the evil spiritual forces in the heavens.

On the wings of God's Word also came phrases from an old hymn. As I continued my walk in the morning stillness, the words and tune played in my mind:

I come to the garden alone,
While the dew is still on the roses.
And the voice I hear, falling on my ear,
The Son of God discloses.
And, He walks with me and He talks with me,
And He tells me I am His own.
And the joy we share as we tarry there,
None other has ever known.
    –"In the Garden" © 1913 by C. Austin Miles

The words of Scripture and the words of song brought hope and peace, which in turn, resurrected a spirit of determination. I recalled the many other tumultuous times of seasons past when God guided me through the emotional tempest, just as he has for thousands of other people. Tears of thankfulness replaced my tears of despair. I was in nature's garden, emotionally-broken, and God had met there.

I eventually returned to the cabin with a smile dawning

204   WALKING IN TRUST

on my face and with Scripture and song in my heart. Sage
was lying on her blanket near the picture window. I hooked
the leash to her collar and coaxed her, with a slight tug, to
follow me. I patted her head gently and whispered in her
ear, even though I knew she could not hear me. "Come on,
girl—we're going squirrel sniffing!"

Unlike her former self, eager to go for a walk, Sage
hesitantly allowed me to lead her out the cabin door and
down the short set of steps. We started with the familiar,
earthen driveway. Firm dirt beneath her feet always provided
confidence to Sage, so we walked the trodden path. The
fresh summer air and light breeze seemed to carry scents
which enticed her, and soon we were walking on the pine-
needled forest floor, away from the well-used path. Sage
sniffed the ground and the pine trunks. Soon her flag tail
waved with the pleasure of a Springer spaniel on a bird hunt!

As we walked back to the cabin, Sage's fur picked up
some prickly grasses, and she shook her body as a dog
does after emerging from water. I brushed her feathery
coat with my hand, loosening some of the stickers, and we
continued our journey. My mind considered the significance
and my heart soared. Life's challenges can come from places
unknown, at unexpected times, liked barbed grasses. I could
choose to shake them off and carry on with life, or I could
let them stick tightly to me, barbs constantly jabbing. I could
also seek God's help in dealing with those prickly problems,
just as I helped Sage deal with the bristles in her fur. In
times past I would allow my emotions to propel me through
the gauntlet of life; now I let Jesus run with me as I declare
the holy Word of God over my circumstances. Instead of
running away from my troubles, I've learned to run to my
Savior, even if that means running to the cabin to meet him
in that special sanctuary he's provided. I may still grow weary
from the *Bam! Pow! Bam!*, but Jesus takes the *Whacks* for

me, just as he did two-thousand years ago. He also lifts the
burdens from my drooping, wearied shoulders, placing them
onto his own, just as he carried the cross on his bloodied,
battered body that day at Calvary.

Sage forged through her own *Whacks*. Most times she
hit a home run with her happy disposition and wagging
tail. But on occasion, Sage wavered, discouraged by circumstances of age and health. Yet, she still found pleasure in
life despite the disabilities that afflicted her, satisfaction in
simple things like woodland walking and squirrel sniffing.
Sage persevered, sometimes with my coaching and coaxing.
I, too, have endured, winging through situations like the
incredible sandhill cranes. And with the help of my Eternal
Coach, I will continue to persevere, following in the paw-
prints of my blind dog.

PRAYER:
Heavenly Father, may the example of your Holy Son's persever-
ance inspire me to pick up the sword of the Spirit in my times of
trial and distress. When life's struggles jab me like prickly barbs,
help me to preen them from my heart and mind, to persevere, so
that I may one day discover the reward of endurance, the ultimate
Home Run—life forever with you! Amen.

Afterword

Sage departed this world on March 24, 2012. She developed cancer and by the time we realized it, nothing could be done. As her heart stopped beating, we said our goodbyes and whispered to her what a delightful, dear dog she had been.

John Newton published the words to the hymn "Amazing Grace" in 1772. Millions still sing this beloved song in churches today. The words, "I once was lost, but now am found; was blind, but now I see" have even deeper meaning for me now, having shared more than a decade with a blind dog who taught me so much about my own faith walk, about walking in trust.

I often imagined Sage to be an angel in disguise, sent by God to teach and to inspire those around her. Sage's visits and her life story encouraged many children to persevere in spite of the hardships and challenges they face. Through the life of a blind springer spaniel, I have learned more fully what it means to walk by faith and not by sight—and I am still growing in that ability.

Sage was my seeing-eye dog of faith. If Sage, with her disability, could exemplify positive life lessons, then with God's help, I believe I can also display those characteristics to others who cross my path.

The word *sage* can mean "one who advises." My blind dog gave advice every day by the way she displayed courage, faith, goodness, patience and perseverance. The Lord encourages us by the Bible, by the example of his Son, Jesus Christ, and the fellowship and help of his Holy Spirit. My hope and prayer is that you also find the same inspiration and thereby discover your own faith increasing as you walk with God and travel life's journey on Earth. May you also see more and more clearly, with the eyes of faith, the One who cannot be seen but who loves us more than we can ever imagine!

Acknowledgments

In honor of Sage, a precious gift from God!

In memory of Dr. Justin Johnson, a talented, incredible veterinarian who was also our friend.

In thanksgiving to my Lord and Savior, Jesus Christ, for his multitude of blessings and his unconditional love and saving grace!

Also, a heartfelt thanks to my parents, Earl and Marcia Mansfield, to my husband, Greg Irwin, and to my plethora of friends, near and far, for your love and encouragement.

And lastly, a special thank you to Catherine Lawton and Christina Slike of Cladach Publishing for their dedicated work, their helpful guidance, and their incredible kindnesses, all of which glorifies God!

Thank you all!

About the Author

Gayle Irwin is a writer, author and speaker with a strong background in animal welfare. Her credentials include work as a journalist and conservation and humane educator. She is the author of two children's books about Sage: *Sage's Big Adventure* and *Sage Learns to Share*. A story about Sage written by Mrs. Irwin appears in *Chicken Soup for the Soul: What I Learned from the Dog* (2009) and *Chicken Soup for the Soul: Finding My Faith* (2012). She has also contributed to other *Chicken Soup for the Soul* editions. Mrs. Irwin writes regularly for *Our Town Casper*, a monthly community magazine, and for *The River Press*, a newspaper in Fort Benton, Montana. She has created educational activity books and other written content for the Upper Missouri River Breaks National Interpretive Center in Montana.

Mrs. Irwin sees God's handiwork in his creation and believes great lessons can be learned by observing nature. She shares those lessons with students and others when she speaks.

Mrs. Irwin was raised in Iowa where she first learned to appreciate God's creation. She currently lives in Casper, Wyoming. She is a member of Wyoming Writers, Inc. for which she creates newsletters and website content, as well as the Society of Children's Book Writers and Illustrators.

Learn more about Mrs. Irwin, her works, and her pets at www.gaylemirwin.com.